Haynes

Build your own
Computer

4th Edition

© Haynes Publishing 2010
First published 2003
Reprinted 2004 (twice)
Second edition published 2005
Reprinted 2006
Third edition published 2007
Fourth edition published March 2010

Published by: Haynes Publishing
Sparkford, Yeovil, Somerset BA22 7JJ, UK
Tel: 01963 442030 Fax: 01963 440001
Int. tel: +44 1963 442030 Fax: +44 1963 440001
E-mail: sales@haynes.co.uk
Website: www.haynes.co.uk

British Library Cataloguing in Publication Data:
A catalogue record for this book is available from the British Library

ISBN 978 1 84425 929 8

Printed in the UK.

Haynes

Build your own **Computer**

4th Edition

Contents

Introduction

Welcome to the fourth edition of our guide to building your own PC. The world of computers has changed dramatically since the first, second and third editions of this book were published: we've moved from Windows XP to Windows Vista and Windows 7, while the familiar Pentium processor has been superseded by dual-core, and even quad-core, processors delivering performance that we could only dream of a few years ago. Most importantly of all, advances in technology and plummeting prices mean that you can build an extremely powerful machine on a very modest budget.

In this manual, we cover two kinds of PC project: a powerful and enormously upgradeable PC that will last you for years and years and a tiny PC that's perfect for putting in your front room – and that delivers an awful lot of power without breaking the bank.

While this book is brand new, you'll find that the important things haven't changed. We keep jargon to a minimum, we explain exactly what components you'll need and where to get them for the best possible price, and of course we provide step-by-step tutorials showing you how to build your PC with the minimum of fuss.

Why do I want to build my own computer?

That's a very good question. After all, few of us build our own houses or our own cars, so why on earth should you build your own computer when you can just buy one from a shop? There are several really good reasons and the most important one is this: If building a car was as easy and as flexible as building a computer, you'd be driving a car that looked like an Aston Martin, handled like a Porsche, had the same luggage space as a Saab Estate, was as quiet as a Lexus and used less petrol than a Toyota Prius.

Building your own computer is the only way to get a perfect PC. So what makes a PC perfect? There are four key criteria. It should fit your needs exactly; it should be flexible; it should be easily expandable; and it should be affordable. Let's look at each of those criteria in more detail.

The perfect PC fits your needs exactly When you buy a ready-made PC, it's likely to be a good all-rounder, and while there's nothing wrong with that it does mean it probably won't be perfect for the things you actually want it to do. While most manufacturers enable you to change various options – so you can specify a slightly bigger hard disk, say, or a slightly better graphics card – the available options are usually fairly limited. For example, manufacturers typically offer two or three different graphics cards on a particular PC, but there are hundreds of such cards out there. It's entirely possible that the right one for you isn't available from that particular manufacturer – or that if the right one is available, the right hard disk isn't, or it doesn't come with the particular processor you'd prefer, or you don't like the look of the PC's case. And so on.

When you build your own PC you don't have to compromise, so if you want a really quick PC that can happily handle video editing, has all the necessary connectors for your cameras and

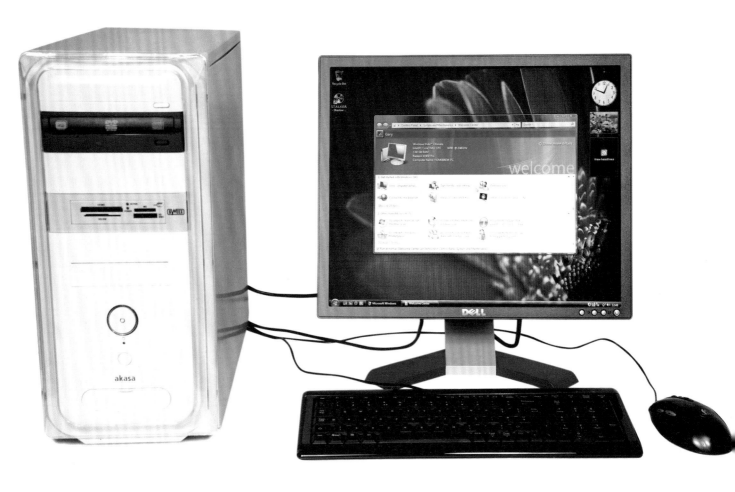

camcorder and doesn't sound like a jumbo jet when you use it then that's what you build. Alternatively, you might want a cheap and cheerful PC that doesn't take up much room, doesn't cost the earth and doesn't bankrupt you when the electricity bill arrives. Once again, if you want it you can build it.

The perfect PC is flexible The days when PCs were used only for dull work things are long gone, and today's PCs should be able to handle anything you can throw at them – managing your digital photos, editing your home movies, playing games, burning DVDs and so on. More importantly, a perfect PC should be able to handle anything you throw at it in the future too, so for example a PC that's struggling with today's games won't be able to handle the latest releases in a year or two. When you build your own PC you can make sure it's not only powerful enough for what you want to do today, but for what you want to do tomorrow too.

The perfect PC is expandable It's impossible to predict what you might want to do in the future. You might not fancy video editing now, but in a year's time you might be making home movies of the kids or even making your own spy thrillers in the shed – at which point you discover that your graphics card really isn't up to the job. Or you might decide to digitise your record collection and store all your albums in MP3 format – and within weeks, your

hard disk is positively packed. With an expandable PC, both problems are easy to solve. In the first scenario, you'd simply pop in a new graphics card and, in the second, you'd add another hard disk. Easy.

The trick to expandability is planning. If you make sure the PC you build today sticks to established industry standards and avoids technologies that are already heading into history, you'll be able to upgrade it easily and affordably for many years to come.

The perfect PC is affordable When you buy a ready-made PC, it's been built to a particular price – and inevitably that means compromises. You might get a free printer but discover that the machine doesn't really have enough memory; it might include a giant monitor but the manufacturer has cut costs elsewhere and installed a graphics card that isn't really up to the job; it might have the Home Basic version of Windows, which is pretty useless compared to the Home Premium edition, and so on.

When you build your own PC, you decide what your PC includes and how much you're willing to pay for it. Shopping around for components can save you a packet and, if you don't go for the very latest processors, you can end up with a PC that's more than capable of doing anything you want it to do without paying premium prices.

Does that sound like your kind of computer? Then read on.

PART

Planning the 'perfect' PC

By doing all the donkey work yourself, you might justly assume that you can build a new computer for less than you'd pay in the shops. The truth may surprise you: you probably can't. But before you return this manual to the bookstore in a fit of pique, consider both the reasons why ... and the reasons why it doesn't matter.

Four good reasons to build your own computer

Original equipment manufacturers (OEMs) – or computer manufacturers, as the rest of us call them – get all of their components at bulk prices, so they pay less for their bits than you will. In some cases, that means building your own computer will cost slightly more than buying one off the shelf, but that's not always the case. There are four key reasons why you should consider building your own rather than buying.

Bargain of the century or a duff deal in disguise? If you've ever browsed the adverts and waded through specs, you'll know just how confusing buying a computer can be. So don't do it. Build one instead.

1. Satisfaction

The second sweetest phrase in the English language is 'I made that' (the sweetest is 'tax rebate'). Building your own computer is an immensely satisfying project. It's fun to do and you end up with a PC that fits your needs exactly.

2. Knowledge

Everybody uses PCs, but how many of them have the faintest idea of how they work? When you build your own, you'll discover how everything fits together, you'll be able to see right through the marketing hype and you'll see where manufacturers cut corners. More importantly, the knowledge you'll gain from building your first PC means that you'll be able to tackle anything from upgrades and repairs to another PC build with complete confidence.

3. Money

Despite what we said above, you really can build a new PC on the cheap. The computing business is rather fashion driven, with hardware firms competing to offer the very latest kit. But the very latest kit comes with prices to match and, six months later, you'll be able to buy the same components for a fraction of the money. Will you really notice the difference between a 2.7GHz and a 2.8GHz processor? The answer is no – but you will notice a big difference in the price of the processors.

The key is compromise – and knowing where you can cut corners and where you definitely shouldn't. A PC with the fastest possible processor but a slow hard disk and inadequate memory will be massively outgunned by one with a slightly slower chip, the right amount of memory and a fast hard disk. By choosing your components carefully, you can build a PC that will out-perform a shop-bought machine in every area that matters to you.

4. It's the only PC you'll ever need

The projects we show you in this book are designed to be future-proof: by sticking to industry-standard technologies and making sure there's adequate room for expansion, both PCs can be upgraded at any time. Not only do you get to design your PC from the ground up to ensure it does precisely what you want it to do, you can also ensure that you can expand, upgrade and enhance your computer more or less forever.

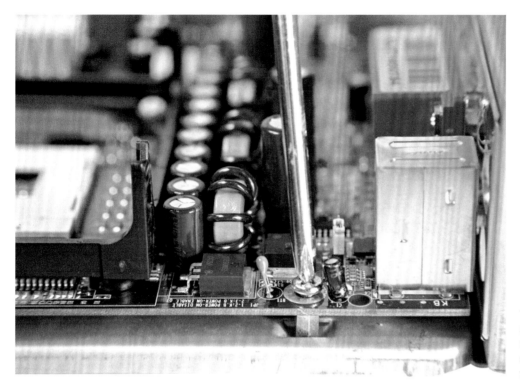

The ultimate upgrade: replacing an outmoded – or broken – motherboard. But rather that, surely, than shelling out on a whole new system.

Pull the other one!

We know what you're thinking: surely all computers become obsolete in a year or so? We'd argue otherwise. Some bits might not suit your needs in a couple of years, so for example you might decide that the graphics card needs beefing up – but changing that is just a matter of popping open the case and putting a better graphics card in. Faster processor? More memory? A TV tuner card? No problem. Has the hard disk packed up? Pull it out and pop another one in.

The key to a future-proof PC is really the motherboard. If you ensure that the motherboard supports technologies that will be around for a good few years, such as Serial ATA for storage and PCI Express for video cards, you can be confident that you'll be able to exchange components at any time. Similarly, if you look for a board that supports not just the processor you plan to buy but the very latest processors Intel or AMD are making, you can be sure you'll be able to upgrade the processor. And if you stick to industry standards such as ATX and Micro ATX motherboards (more of them later) then one day you'll be able to replace the motherboard and re-use the hard disk, DVD drive, case and power supply. It's almost always cheaper to upgrade a PC than replace it and it's more environmentally friendly too.

When we said that the computer industry was very like the fashion industry, we meant it. Computers are sold in much the same way as designer handbags, with new must-have models emerging every few months. There's nothing wrong with the old handbags and there's nothing wrong with a computer that isn't at the absolute cutting edge either. We're long past the point where

computers struggled to keep up with us, and these days a very slightly faster processor isn't going to make your Facebook updates funnier, your internet connection faster or junk emails any less annoying – but computer firms would like you to think so, because their profits depend on it.

Put it this way: would you buy a car and replace it every year, losing thousands in depreciation and sending a perfectly good vehicle to the scrapyard just because there's a new model with slightly different wing mirrors? Of course you wouldn't. So why do it with a PC?

So what's the downside?

Are there any negatives to building your own PC? We don't think so. It takes a bit more research than buying a ready-made PC off the shelf and, if you're looking for the best prices, you might end up getting your components from five or six different suppliers but that's not a huge problem. The big downside is that a retail PC comes with technical support and consumer protection – if you get it home and it doesn't work, or something fails within a few weeks, the manufacturer will fix it. But when you buy components, you're protected under the Sale of Goods Act and manufacturers' warranties, so if they pack up unexpectedly you're still covered.

As for technical support, when you've built your PC, you'll be able to fix any problems yourself – usually in a matter of minutes. That's much less hassle than having to send your machine off and managing without it for days or even weeks while the manufacturer fixes it.

PART How to shop

There's no particular mystery to PCs: they're all made with components that you can buy on the open market. While the specifics differ from machine to machine, almost all PCs are made of the following bits:

An OEM would scoff at pretty packaging but there's a lot to be said for a retail product that gives you everything you need in the box. A motherboard, for instance, should include hard and floppy drive cables, a heatsink retention frame, installation screws, an I/O shield, chipset drivers, a manual and a warranty.

- a case
- a power supply
- a motherboard
- a processor
- memory
- storage
- a sound card
- a video card

All of these things are widely available, and the only thing you can't get in a typical computer shop is a case that's identical to a specific manufacturer's one – so if you want to build something that looks identical to Apple's iMac or a particular Dell, you're out of luck. However, in the marketplace you'll find all kinds of cases ranging from traditional desktops to stylish-looking, ultra-slim designs that look great sitting under your TV. When you build your PC the problem isn't finding components: quite the reverse. You'll be spoilt for choice.

OEM versus retail

When you build your own computer, the acronym OEM will save you a lot of money. OEM is short for Original Equipment Manufacturer and you can find OEM versions of almost anything. So what are OEM versions and why should you seek them out? In a word: money.

When you buy a copy of Windows in a shop, the package includes a nice box and technical support. If you buy the OEM version it comes in a plain white box and you don't get technical support – but you don't pay as much money, either. For example, as we write this, the Home Premium edition of Windows Vista is £133.97 in most online shops. The OEM version, an identical piece of software, is £86.13. The only important difference is that OEM versions aren't transferable, so if you replace your computer in a few years you won't be able to transfer your copy of Windows.

It's a similar story with hardware. OEM versions of hard disks, DVD drives and other components don't come in smart packaging, don't include lots of bundled goodies and tend to come in a plain cardboard box, if they come in a box at all. The last time we bought an OEM hard disk and DVD drive, they were wrapped in bubble wrap and sellotaped shut. They were also around 20% cheaper than the retail versions. Who needs boxes?

Technically, we mere mortals aren't supposed to get our hands on OEM products, but you'll find them everywhere: online retailers such as Dabs.com, specialist PC shops and computer fairs. Provided you're willing to obtain your own cables, fittings, software and other bits and bobs (depending on the case and motherboard you buy, you might not even need to do that), OEM products offer very good value for money indeed.

When a power supply unit's air vents looks like this, you can be sure it has been round the block a few times. Nothing a blast of compressed air won't clear, of course, but you have to wonder how much life it has left.

New versus second hand

Sites such as eBay offer all kinds of components for knock-down prices but, while there are bargains to be had, we'd recommend treading carefully. A second-hand hard disk might well work for years, but equally it could fail within five minutes – and, of course, when you buy second-hand there isn't a warranty.

If you'd rather not buy brand-new bits there are two alternatives: refurbished stock and end-of-line stock. The former has been returned with a fault and fixed by the manufacturer, which can no longer sell it as a brand new item. Instead, the stock is sold as 'refurbished', with a short warranty and a bargain basement price. Prices are close to second-hand prices and a short warranty is better than no warranty.

The second option is end-of-line stock, which firms such as Morgan Computers specialise in. Whenever a firm brings out a new model and stops selling the old version, all that stock has to go somewhere. In many cases it goes to a firm, such as Morgan, that piles the stock high and sells it cheap.

A third option is a combination of refurbished and OEM stock. So-called 'B-grade stock' can include damaged goods that have since been repaired, items in perfect order that were returned without all the manuals and packaging, end-of-line components, used machines dumped by big firms as they replace their computing kit . . . if it works but isn't quite perfect then it's B-grade stock. You won't get much of a warranty – 90 days is good, 30 days more likely – but you are covered by the Sale of Goods Act. Manufacturers must detail what's wrong with the item and if it isn't as described then you're entitled to get your money back. Be careful what you buy, though: a water- or fire-damaged monitor or power supply isn't a safe bet, but a graphics card whose manual has been misplaced could be.

The trick to minimising your budget is to know what corners to cut. We wouldn't recommend saving money by buying a motherboard with limited upgrade options or a hard disk that you'll fill in a fortnight, but you can keep your costs down by choosing refurbished, end-of-line or second-hand components, such as keyboards, mice and monitors.

HP Vectra VEi8 P3-500 128mg Sony 17" Trintron	£195.00	Buy it Now
DELL PIII-450 128MB 6.4GB CD SND **£104.00**	£104.00	Buy it Now
COMPAQ PIII-500 INTERNET READY +15" MONITOR	£135.00	Buy it Now
Pentium 3 Tower System DVD CDRW 17" & more	£200.00	14
Dell P-III 733 Bargain, 256MB, SFF, Dont Miss	£129.99	Buy it Now
HP Vectra VL18 SFF System & 17" Sony T'tron	£104.00	18
P3 FULL Tower Server DVD CDRW 768Meg 19"	£170.10	15
MEGA VALUE PC, MONITOR, WINDOWS XP & FREE P&P	£399.00	Buy it Now

Older but still-functional computers are regularly replaced by individuals and industry alike. Shop around at an online auction site like eBay and you'll certainly find some bargains. Look out for pitfalls, though: an office-based machine may lack a sound card and speakers, and you should check whether the hard disk has been wiped clean of software.

PART  Where to buy

When you want to buy computer kit, there's no shortage of firms after your cash. These are the main types.

Superstores like PC World offer a good selection of DIY components alongside complete computer systems. Check the Bargain Zones for the best deals.

Computer superstores

Superstores are aimed at a fairly narrow group of customers: people who want to buy a ready-made computer or who need a replacement or upgrade for an existing machine. With the exception of special offers, prices tend to be on the high side and they're usually undercut by online-only vendors – although some chains are now offering the same prices in their shops as they do online, which makes things more competitive.

High street independents

Independent computer shops are a mixed bunch in our experience, so while many small shops are staffed by friendly, knowledgeable people who happily offer advice, many aren't. A good independent can be a great ally when it comes to all things computing, but such independents can be hard to find.

Mail order and online

Mail order and internet companies don't need to pay expensive high street rents or employ lots of staff, so they can offer much keener prices than shops – typically up to 30% lower – as well as B-grade stock and OEM products that high street chains can't sell. It's not always clear whether such firms are selling retail or OEM products, so always check that you're ordering the right thing. Watch out for delivery charges too, as they can add a big chunk to the price.

Dabs.com is one of the largest online high-tech retailers in the UK. Its extensive Dabsvalue range includes unbranded OEM-style products at rock-bottom prices.

Computer fairs

Computer fairs are regular events all over the country. Here you'll find some of the UK's lowest prices, provided you're willing to haggle a little. Typically you'll find a selection of OEM products, end-of-line products and individual components scavenged from older PCs, making such fairs a great place to find almost anything for building or repairing a computer.

If it's your first visit to a computer fair, we'd suggest leaving your wallet at home. Note the names of traders you're interested in, get a feel for the prices and then go home and see if they're competitive. Official, monthly fairs are well policed by the organisers and regular traders do tend to be trustworthy, but like any such event there may be a few less reliable types. If you follow the golden rules, you should be okay:

- Only deal with traders who openly display a landline number – not just a mobile number – and a postal address.
- Establish with the trader what your return rights are and how you would return faulty goods – and do it before handing over any money.
- Keep all packaging and receipts.

No matter what you're looking for or what kind of retailer you prefer, it's important to shop around. Prices for components can vary widely, often for no apparent reason. If you're shopping online, use shop search engines, such as Google's Products (**www.google.co.uk/products**) and Kelkoo (**www.kelkoo.com**), to compare prices and watch out for sneaky tactics, such as sites that automatically select the most expensive delivery option by default. Most importantly of all, pay by credit card to take advantage of fraud protection and consumer protection and make sure you're aware of your consumer rights in the event of any problems. See Appendix 4 for contact information and useful resources.

Snapping up bargains at a computer fair stall. See Appendix 4 for details of websites that list local markets.

PART

Hard and soft options

In the next section, we'll look at the main components that go together to make a computer. But first you must decide what type of computer you wish to build.

Matching hardware to software

If there was a magic formula – 'to do X and Y buy Z' – we would print it here. Sadly there isn't – but then you can't just walk into a shop and buy the 'perfect PC' straight off the shelf. Nor can we provide you with a definitive buying guide or make specific product recommendations. For one thing, any such advice would be instantly out of date; for another, one of the great secrets of computer design is that it matters far, far less which brand name you buy than whether a given component adheres to industry standards (no proprietary parts here, thank you very much) and has the right specification for its intended purpose. As a system-builder, you have the opportunity – nay, the luxury – of being able to make informed choices about every single part of your computer.

We will talk you through the hardware in Part 2. However, the old adage of horses for courses holds true in the software stakes too: the computer you build must be well-suited to its end use. You don't need a room-sized mainframe to surf the web any more than you need seven satellite speakers and a sub-woofer to keep track of your household finances, but you do need a good deal of processing power and a swanky video card if you want to play computer games (plus a joystick, a powerful sound card and probably a set of headphones to keep the neighbours sweet).

Recommended system requirements

Application type	Typical example	Processor speed (MHz)	Memory (MB)	Hard disk space (MB)	Other requirements
Operating system	Windows Vista Home Basic	1,000 (1GHz)	512	15,000 (15GB)	
Office applications	Microsoft Office 2007 Home and Student Edition	500	256	1,500 (1.5GB)	
Image editor	Jasc Paint Shop Pro	500	128	75	
DVD movie player	CyberLink PowerDVD	400	64	40	DVD drive
Digital video editor	Pinnacle Studio 9	800	512	500	FireWire/USB port to connect a camcorder; lots of hard disk space for storing raw video
Digital media	Roxio Creator 7	500	256	1,000	Recordable CD or DVD drive
Game	Medal of Honor: Pacific Assault	1,500	512	3,000	Video card with 128MB memory
Desktop publishing	CorelDRAW Graphics Suite 12	200	128	250	
Reference	Encyclopaedia Britannica 2004	350	256	400	
Antivirus	Norton Antivirus 2005	300	128	125	
Utility suite	Norton SystemWorks 2005	300	128	150	

In all cases, we assume the presence of a monitor, mouse, keyboard, sound card, speakers, a CD drive from which to install the software and an internet connection.

Changing pace

Computer hardware and software have long played a game of catch-up with one another but not always in the same direction. A few years ago, for instance, it was common for software applications to stretch hardware capability to breaking point. This was especially true in the realm of gaming. Then, for a while, hardware performance leapt ahead and the average desktop PC was much more powerful than we actually needed it to be. Real multitasking, by which we mean being able to run several intensive applications simultaneously, became the norm. Even the humblest mass-production shop-bought system could handle having a web browser, e-mail program, word processor, encyclopaedia and desktop publishing program all open at the same time with surplus capacity aplenty.

By and large, the power balance has shifted little. To make the point, we've listed a few typical applications along with their recommended hardware specifications in the table on p.16. Now, nothing here will remotely stretch any PC that you're liable to buy or build today. Indeed, only one of our sample applications specifies so much as a 1.5GHz processor – they're currently running upwards of twice as fast – and you're unlikely to be pushed for hard disk space with today's drives with hundreds or even thousands of gigabytes of storage. The game's requirement for a hefty video card is the only potential sticking point.

Memory matters

But it's not *quite* as straightforward as all that. Perhaps the most noticeable and certainly the most significant thing about these figures is the importance of memory. The overall quantity of RAM in a system – and to a lesser extent the *type* of RAM chosen – has a huge bearing on that system's overall performance, especially when it comes to multitasking. It's one thing for a computer to run 17 programs at the same time but quite another for it to do so smoothly without locking-up or hanging the system. Given that multitasking is a PC's forte, or should be, and that you shouldn't have to shut down programs A and B before firing up programs C, D and E, it's sensible to install considerably more RAM than you think you need in order to keep things ticking along nicely. Compromise in almost every other area before skimping on memory.

Processors matter too

Moreover, these system requirements mask the fact that in certain key areas software is now once again pushing at the boundaries of hardware. Computer gaming is one obvious area where it's beneficial if not downright essential to have a fast processor, stacks of memory and the very latest souped-up video card at your disposal. Anything less and you won't see your games play to their full potential. Frame rates drop and detail is lost.

But even if you're not interested in games, consider digital video. This is another key area where the possibilities can be hampered by hardware limitations. For instance, a PC makes a fabulous video editing suite if you have a camcorder. You can transfer raw footage to the hard disk and tweak and transform it into a polished home movie. You can then publish your efforts on a website, share them via e-mail or make your own DVDs. Even basic video editing software is spectacularly powerful (including Windows Movie Maker, which comes free with Windows XP and Vista). For the amateur film-maker, these are happy days. However, the harsh reality is that you need pretty sturdy hardware to work with digital video at a comfortable pace. Just about any PC can edit and produce a movie, but not all can do it while you wait. A slow system will take hours to render a movie (i.e. apply your edits, captions, effects and so forth to raw footage and produce a finished file), and some will need all night and perhaps well into the following morning. While it's engaged in the business of rendering, there's not much else you can do with your computer short of chivvying it along with words of encouragement or, more likely, frustration.

If movie-making appeals, don't skimp on processing power.

Bottom line: if video is your thing, invest in a speedy processor to cut the waiting time to a minimum.

Beige be gone

Much to the amusement of Mac fans, for whom form is almost as important as function, most PC manufacturers now have a stab at making their products attractive. Usually, they fail dismally, but you, the system builder, can have a much better go at this yourself.

We'll build two very different PCs in the course of this book, one of which would look perfectly at home in a living room setting. This is an example of a 'small form factor' PC, which is what you'll likely want if you intend to build a home entertainment centre.

A what, you wonder? Well, odd though it may sound, a suitably configured PC connected to a TV can effectively replace your video recorder, DVD player, stereo system and games console. It can also showcase digital images, import and export media to and from other computers in a home network, and generally function as the very hub of your home entertainment. Forget the keyboard and mouse; all you need is a remote control. Skip to Appendix 2 now for more details. Meanwhile, just bear in mind as you go along that the PC has finally made the leap from the study to the sitting room. You are in the enviable position of being able to design and build an ideal system from scratch.

Our other project PC caters more for future expansion and flexibility but it's no mean looker for all that. It would also be ideally suited to the next step in system-building, which is customising or 'modding' (modifying) a PC for maximum effect. We're talking cut-away Perspex panels that showcase internal neon tube lights, swish water-cooling systems, solid gold heatsinks and that kind of thing. This, though, is subject matter for a different book.

But we're getting ahead of ourselves. Let's turn now to the nuts and bolts that you will use to build your computer.

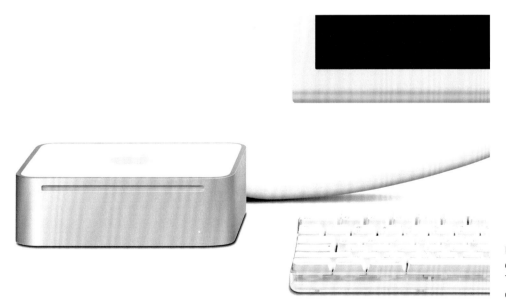

Even now, not many PCs can compete with a Mac for styling. Then again, you can't build your own Mac.

PART  # Choosing your hardware

Inevitably this section gets a little bit technical but, as always, we focus on what you need to know instead of getting bogged down in jargon and the inner workings of electronics. You don't need to know the history of processors to appreciate that a top-end, multi-core processor is great for heavy-duty applications but completely over the top for browsing the web and replying to emails.

PART 2 Motherboard

The motherboard is the heart of your system and the single most important piece of hardware you will buy. Everything else connects to it: the processor plugs into it, your hard disk and DVD drive connect to it, the memory modules plug into its memory slots and, in some cases, it might even include your graphics and sound card. When you buy a PC from a shop, you probably don't pay any attention to the motherboard beyond knowing that it's there and it works. When you build a system from scratch, however, it must be your primary consideration. The motherboard you choose dictates the hard disk you can install, the kind and speed of processor you can use and even the kind of case you can put your computer into.

A sample motherboard

Here's a close look at a motherboard like the one we'll be using in the first of our projects.

Memory slots	For installing memory modules
Processor socket	For installing the processor
Chipset (Northbridge)	The motherboard's control centre
Parallel	For connecting a printer
PS/2 (2)	For connecting a mouse and keyboard
S/PDIF in/out	For importing and exporting digital audio signals
RJ45 (2)	For connecting a wired local area network (LAN)
USB (4)	For connecting peripheral devices
Audio (6)	For connecting speakers (7.1 surround sound), a line-in device and a microphone
Wi-Fi	For connecting a wireless networking receiver
PCI Express 16x	For installing a video card

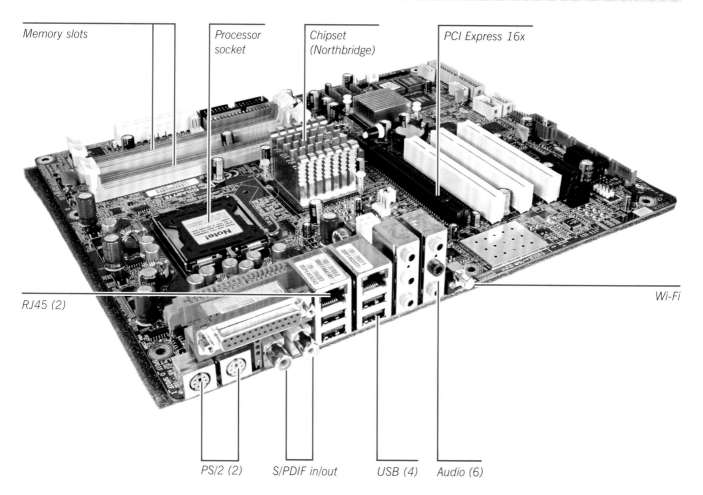

Memory slots — Processor socket — Chipset (Northbridge) — PCI Express 16x

RJ45 (2)

Wi-Fi

PS/2 (2) — S/PDIF in/out — USB (4) — Audio (6)

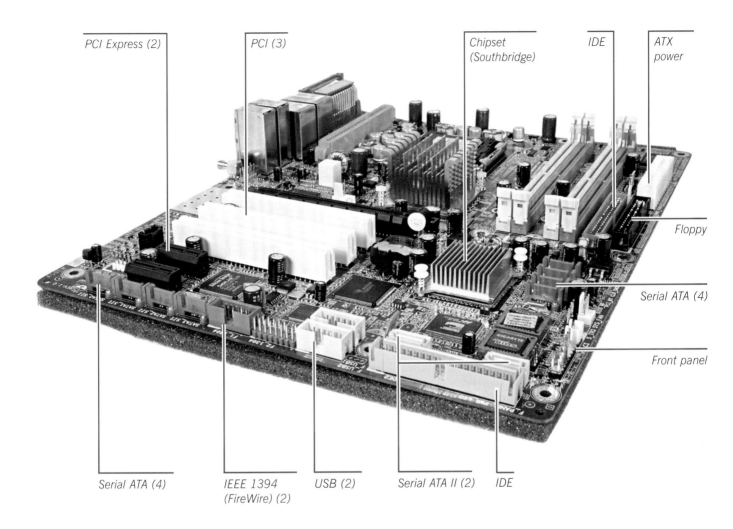

PCI Express (2)   PCI (3)   Chipset (Southbridge)   IDE   ATX power

Floppy

Serial ATA (4)

Front panel

Serial ATA (4)   IEEE 1394 (FireWire) (2)   USB (2)   Serial ATA II (2)   IDE

QUICK Q&A

I'm considering a motherboard that claims to be 'legacy-free'. It sounds like a bonus but what does it mean?

It means it has no serial, parallel, mouse or keyboard ports and nowhere to connect a floppy disk drive! This might be a good thing but only if you already have or intend to get a USB mouse, keyboard, printer, etc. and don't mind going without a floppy drive. It's certainly the way of the future. For this project, we couldn't quite bring ourselves to ditch these legacy interfaces just yet.

PCI (3)	For installing standard expansion cards
PCI Express (2)	For installing the latest, fastest expansion cards
Serial ATA (8)	For connecting new-style hard drives
IEEE 1394 (FireWire) (2)	For connecting via a FireWire cable to a drive or device
USB (2)	For connecting via a USB cable to a drive or device
Serial ATA II (2)	For connecting high-speed new-style hard drives
IDE (2)	For connecting old-style hard drives
Front panel	For connecting lights and buttons on the front of the case
Chipset (Southbridge)	The motherboard's control centre
Floppy	For connecting a floppy drive
ATX power	For connecting the power supply unit

And another one

This motherboard is an older model but representative of the kind of thing you could easily pick up for a song at a computer fair. We've highlighted the key differences.

AGP	This special slot is used to install the video card. Gradually, the AGP standard is being superseded by the superior PCI Express standard.
PCI	This motherboard has six PCI slots for adding expansion cards, whereas the newer model on the previous pages has but three. However, the newer model also has two PCI Express slots which can host faster, more powerful expansion cards. It also has both wired (LAN) and wireless (Wi-Fi) connections built-in, plus a powerful on-board multi-channel audio chip with a stack of inputs and outputs. This means that you simply don't need as many expansion cards.
Processor socket	Here we see a Socket 478 socket for a Pentium 4 processor. On the newer motherboard, this has been replaced by the LGA775 Pentium 4 socket. As we shall see, the design of processor sockets (and, before that, slots) is ever-changing, which generates a whole bunch of compatibility issues.

Memory slots	The difference here is not obvious to the eye but the newer motherboard can run memory in dual-channel configuration whereas this model can not. For the benefits, see p.41.
IDE	There are two IDE sockets on this motherboard, each of which can host two hard drives or optical CD/DVD drives. The computer can thus have a maximum of four internal drives. On the new model, we still find the IDE sockets, but these are rapidly disappearing in favour of the Serial ATA standard (for which there are no fewer than ten sockets). It's useful to have an IDE socket or two around, if only for reusing existing hard or optical drives, but SATA is the way forward.

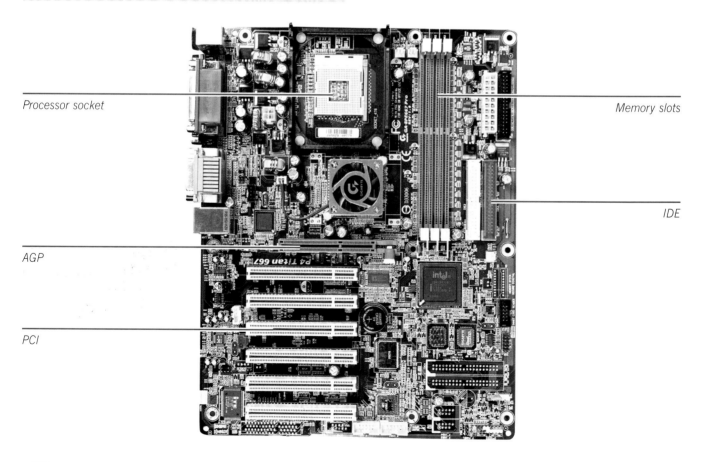

Processor socket

Memory slots

AGP

IDE

PCI

Form factor

This is a fancy way of describing a motherboard's size and shape, important because it involves industry-wide standards and ties in with the computer case and power supply. Form factors have evolved through the years, culminating since 1995 in a popular and flexible standard known as ATX. Not just one ATX standard, of course: there are MiniATX, MicroATX and FlexATX motherboards out there, all progressively slimmed-down versions of full-size ATX. The upside of a smaller motherboard is that you can use a smaller case and reduce the overall dimensions of your computer; the downside is a corresponding reduction in expandability. A full-sized ATX motherboard can have up to seven expansion slots while a MicroATX motherboard is limited to four.

Should you have a tape measure handy and wish to do some checking, here are the maximum ATX motherboard board sizes as specified by Intel:

ATX	305mm	x	244mm
MiniATX	284mm	x	208mm
MicroATX	244mm	x	244mm
FlexATX	229mm	x	191mm

One technical benefit of ATX over the earlier BabyAT form factor from which it directly evolved is that full-length expansion cards can now be fitted in all slots; previously, the location of the processor and memory on the motherboard meant that some slots could only take stumpy (not a technical term) cards. Another is the use of a double-height input/output panel that lets motherboard manufacturers build-in more integrated features. All in all, it's a definite improvement.

But from your point of view, the main attraction has to be the guarantee that any ATX motherboard, including the smaller versions, will fit inside any ATX computer case. That's the beauty of standards.

The most recent mainstream addition to the form factor parade is BTX (Balanced Technology Extended). This has a leaner, flatter form factor compared to ATX, and is specifically designed to facilitate adequate cooling in smaller computers, especially those designed for home entertainment. A BTX motherboard comes in three variations:

BTX	267mm	x	325mm
MicroBTX	267mm	x	263mm
PicoBTX	267mm	x	203mm

Beyond BTX, you can also buy Mini-ITX motherboards from a manufacturer called VIA (**www.viaembedded.com**). These are square in shape, 170mm x 170mm, and designed primarily for squeezing into strictly non-standard computer projects. As Wikipedia (**http://en.wikipedia.org/wiki/Mini-itx**) puts it:

Enthusiasts soon noticed the advantages of small size, low noise and power consumption, and started to push the boundaries of case modding into something else – building computers into nearly every object imaginable, and sometimes even creating new cases altogether. Hollowed out vintage computers, humidors, toys, electronics, musical instruments, and even a 1960s-era toaster have become homes to relatively quiet, or even silent Mini-ITX systems, capable of many of the tasks of a modern desktop PC.

For examples and inspiration, see **www.mini-itx.com**.

Next in line comes the even smaller 120mm x 120mm Nano-ITX form factor. Like Mini-ITX, this is developed exclusively by VIA with the aim of making even smaller, but still fully functional, PCs possible.

A really very tiny indeed 12cm-square Nano-ITX motherboard from VIA.

The chipset

The real meat of a motherboard resides in its chipset: a collection of microchips that together control all the major functions. Without a chipset, a motherboard would be lifeless; with a duff chipset, it may be inadequate for your needs. Indeed, as one motherboard manufacturer explained it to us, the chipset *is* the motherboard: don't ask what this or that motherboard can do – ask instead what chipset it uses and there you'll find your answer.

So what does a chipset do, precisely? Well, at one level it controls the flow of data between motherboard components through a series of interfaces. Each interface, or channel, is called a bus. The most important buses are:

FSB (Front Side Bus) The interface between the Northbridge component of the chipset and the processor.

Memory bus The interface between the chipset and RAM.

AGP (Accelerated Graphics Port) The interface between the chipset and the AGP port. This is gradually disappearing from motherboards as more and more video cards are designed for the PCI Express slot.

PCI (Peripheral Component Interconnect) bus The interface between the chipset and PCI expansion slots. Pretty much any expansion card can be installed here, including sound cards, network cards and TV tuners. The exception is a video card, as these are, or were, designed for the higher bandwidth AGP interface. Like AGP, PCI is gradually giving way to PCI Express.

PCI Express bus The interface between the chipset and PCI Express expansion slots. There may be two separate buses determined by the bandwidth of the slots. For instance, the motherboard may have a 16-speed PCI Express slot for the video card and one or more slower slots for standard expansion cards.

IDE (Integrated Drive Electronics) bus The interface between the chipset and hard/optical drives.

SATA (Serial Advanced Technology Attachment) bus An alternative interface between the chipset and hard/optical drives which will eventually completely replace the IDE bus.

And then there are buses controlling the floppy disk drive, parallel and serial ports, USB and FireWire, integrated audio, and more.

Here we have a Pentium 4 processor (left), an 82925XE Northbridge or Memory Controller Hub chip (top right) and an ICR6H Southbridge or Input/Output Controller Hub chip. Which is quite some mouthful. But put them together and you'll have a motherboard with an Intel 925XE chipset.

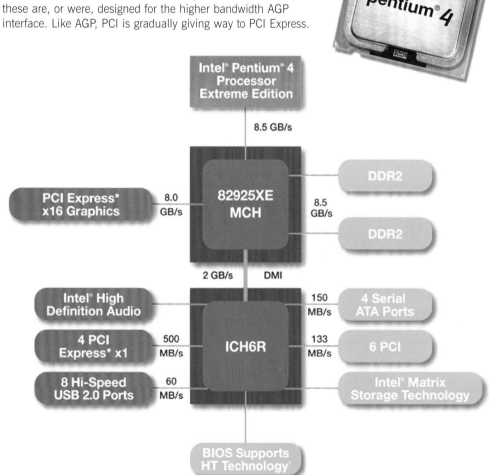

The same chipset viewed schematically. Note how the Northbridge (MCH) and Southbridge (ICH) chips have different responsibilities.

Bus bandwidths

Not all buses are equal. Far from it, in fact: they operate at different speeds and have different 'widths'. For example, the basic single-speed (1x) AGP specification has a clock speed of 66.6MHz (usually expressed as 66MHz). This means that over 66 million units of data can pass between the video card and the chipset through the bus per second. However, the AGP bus transfers 32 bits of data (that's 32 individual 1s and 0s) with every clock cycle, so the true measure of the bus is not its speed alone but rather the overall rate at which data is transferred. This is known as the bandwidth of a bus. In this case, 32 bits pass through the bus 66 million times per second. This equates to a bandwidth of 266MB/sec.

Just to be clear, using round figures, here's the sum:

*66,600,000 clock cycles x 32 bits =
2,131,200,000 bits/sec
There are 8 bits in a byte (B), so this equals
266,400,000B/sec
There are 1,000 bytes in a kilobyte (KB),
so this equals 266,400KB/sec
There are 1,000 kilobytes in a megabyte (MB),
so this equals 266MB/sec*

Looked at another way, the AGP bus transfers sufficient data to fill a recordable CD every three seconds.

It's also possible to run the AGP bus up to eight times faster, which boosts the bandwidth to over 2 gigabytes per sec. This is the kind of speed you need for playing games. By contrast, the PCI bus runs at only 133MB/sec. This is fine for many purposes but not for three-dimensional video.

Now consider the bandwidth of an 800MHz front side bus on a motherboard designed for a Pentium 4 processor. The bus itself is 64 bits wide – that is, 64 bits are transferred every second – and the clock 'ticks' 800 million times per second. This equates to a bandwidth of 6,400MB/sec, or very nearly fast enough to fill a DVD with data in a second.

Some buses can transfer data two, four or eight times per clock cycle, which effectively doubles, quadruples, etc. the overall bandwidth. The new PCI Express standard allows for multiple 'lanes' which pump data in a number of simultaneous streams. The upshot is that PCI Express is vastly superior to that of PCI or even AGP 8x-speed.

If all this makes your head spin, put away your calculator and consult the following table instead.

Some bus bandwidths

	Bus name	Bandwidth (MB/sec)
FSB (Pentium 4 and Core Duo)	400MHz	3,200
	533MHz	4,266
	800MHz	6,400
	1,066MHz	8,500
Expansion slots	PCI	133
	AGP	266
	AGP 2x	533
	AGP 4x	1,066
	AGP 8x	2,133
	PCI Express 1x	500
	PCI Express 2x	1,000
	PCI Express 4x	2,000
	PCI Express 8x	4,000
	PCI Express 16x	8,000
Drive interfaces	IDE/ATA-33	33
	IDE/ATA-66	66
	IDE/ATA-100	100
	IDE/ATA-133	133
	SATA I	150
	SATA II	300

Chipset architecture

We needn't linger on the physical design of chipsets except to comment briefly on the terminology you are likely to encounter:
- **Northbridge** The primary chip in a chipset, it typically controls the processor, memory and video buses.
- **Southbridge** A second chip that typically incorporates the PCI, IDE/SATA and USB buses.
- **Super I/O** A third, subsidiary chip that usually supports the floppy disk drive, serial ports and a parallel port, and sometimes also the mouse and keyboard ports.

However, these associations between bus and chip are far from immutable. Moreover, Intel recently switched to a 'hub architecture' where the Northbridge chip is called the Memory Controller Hub and the Southbridge is the I/O Controller Hub. AMD, that other processor-producing giant, refers to Northbridge and Southbridge chips as the System Controller and Peripheral Bus Controller respectively. More importantly, the latest Athlon 64 processor family incorporates the memory controller within the processor, thereby releasing the Northbridge chip from much of its responsibility.

From the buyer's perspective, it matters more what a chipset offers overall than how it does it.

Processor and memory support

The most important thing about any motherboard is what kind of processor it supports. For example, if you want to build a machine with an Intel Core 2 Duo processor, you'll need a motherboard with a Socket 775 connector because the Core 2 Duo simply won't fit, let alone work, in a motherboard with a different kind of connector. Similarly if you want to use an AMD Opteron quad-core processor, you'll need a motherboard with an AMD AM2 socket. That means it makes a lot of sense to think about motherboard–processor combinations (and price) from the get-go, as they will dictate every other component you purchase.

Once you've looked at processor support, you'll also need to investigate memory support including supported standards, speeds, how many memory slots there are and whether the motherboard supports dual-channel memory modules. We'll cover all of this shortly.

Just to make things a little bit more complicated, Intel makes its own chipsets, so it's extremely easy to compare motherboards compatible with Intel processors, but AMD lets third-party

A Socket 939 Athlon 64 processor.

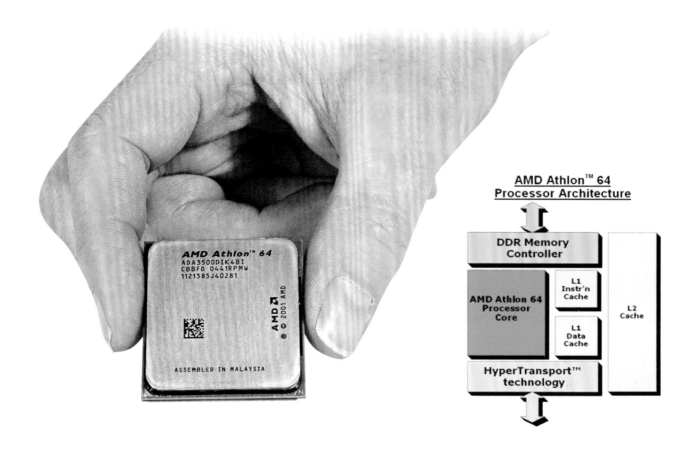

manufacturers develop their own designs. There's nothing wrong with that – in fact, it means there's a huge range of AMD-compatible motherboards to choose from at every price point – but it does make motherboard comparisons slightly trickier.

Integrated multimedia

Until very recently, the question 'should I buy a motherboard with integrated graphics and sound?' had a simple answer, 'No. They're rubbish.' And they were. While motherboards with integrated sound and graphics cards saved you a bit of money – because you didn't need to buy separate sound and video cards – they tended to deliver very basic features, so for example many integrated graphics cards struggled to deliver sufficient horsepower for Windows Vista's pretty, semi-transparent interface.

While there are still plenty of such motherboards in the market, manufacturers appear to have wised up and it's now possible to buy motherboards with rather powerful video cards built-in. As you'll discover in Part 4, a £40–60 motherboard, such as Asus's

M3N78-VM (sorry, that's its name), includes a graphics card that's powerful enough to display high-definition video. Most motherboards now include decent high-definition sound cards too.

So should you consider a motherboard with integrated sound and video? The short answer is 'it depends'. It will certainly save you money, it enables you to cram a PC into a smaller space (stand-alone graphics cards need plenty of room, so if you're building a really small PC then integrated graphics is your only choice) and if you choose your motherboard carefully you won't end up with something that's hopelessly underpowered. However, if you want ultimate performance then stand-alone graphics cards are still much more powerful than their integrated equivalents. If you think integrated video will be fine for now, make sure your motherboard has a spare AGP or PCI Express slot for a graphics card. That means if you want something more powerful later on, you'll be able to slot in a new graphics card without having to replace the entire motherboard.

When both video and audio output are embedded on the motherboard, as in this small form factor example, the need for expansion slots is reduced. In fact, you may get away with none at all.

Sizing up the specifications

On first glance, the specifications of motherboards are written entirely in gibberish – so let's look at two examples and translate everything into English.

Asus P5Q-E

Form factor	ATX	ATX is the 'classic' size of motherboard for desktop PCs.
Processor socket	LGA775	LGA775, also known as Socket 775, is the standard connector for Intel processors, from the Pentium to the Core 2 Quad.
Processor compatibility	Pentium Dual Core Celeron Celeron Dual Core Core 2 Duo Core 2 Extreme Core 2 Quad	This motherboard supports a really good range of Intel processors, from the dual-core Pentium (not the older, single-core Pentiums) to the quad-core Core 2 Quad processor – so it's fairly future-proof.
Supported RAM	DDR2	DDR2 is the most common kind of RAM currently available, which means it's easy to find and it's reasonably cheap.
Maximum RAM	16GB	This motherboard supports more memory than most: the typical motherboard supports up to 8GB.
Supported RAM speeds	PC2-5300 PC2-6400 PC2-8500 PC2-9600	When you buy your memory modules, these are the numbers that matter. The bigger the number, the faster the memory – although to take advantage of PC2-9600 memory, you'll need to use the fastest processors too.
Integrated video	n/a	You'll need to buy a video card if you plump for this one.
Integrated audio	High Definition Audio	No need to buy a sound card: this has a good quality one built in, with surround sound support.
Expansion slots	1 x PCI Express 16 2 x PCI Express x1 2 x PCI Express 2.0 2 x PCI	You'll need a PCI Express 16 slot to install a cutting-edge graphics card, while the PCI Express 2.0 slot means you'll be able to install next-generation cards (PCIE 2.0 is the latest version of the PCI standard). The PCI Express x1 and plain old PCI slots are for installing older add-on cards.
Storage interfaces	1 x ATA 8 x SATA 1 x eSATA	ATA is the interface for older hard disks, but these days the ones to go for are Serial ATA (SATA). An eSATA interface is for external SATA devices that use the eSATA standard.
Other ports	12 x USB 2 x FireWire 2 x Gigabit Ethernet	USB ports are necessary for connecting keyboards, printers and so on, while FireWire is for faster devices such as high-definition cameras. Unusually this motherboard has two network ports: most motherboards have one.

Now that we've translated everything into plain English, it's a lot less intimidating. In the above example we know that the motherboard supports Intel, not AMD processors, and that we can use anything from a dual-core Pentium 4 up to a Core 2 Quad processor – which covers all the basics from cheap and cheerful to blisteringly fast. We don't need a sound card but we do need a video card, the motherboard supports modern SATA hard disks and storage devices, and when we buy memory we need to look for PC2-5300, PC2-6400, PC2-8500 or PC2-9600 memory modules. It supports the latest graphics cards, the older ones and the just-coming-out PCI Express 2.0 graphics cards, and its standard ATX size means it'll fit in a standard ATX case.

Let's look at another motherboard from the same company.

Asus M3N78-VM

Form factor	Micro ATX	Micro ATX is smaller than traditional ATX motherboards, enabling you to put this motherboard in a smaller case.
Processor socket	AM2+	Socket AM2+ is used by AMD processors. You can't use an Intel processor in this motherboard.
Processor compatibility	Athlon 64 Athlon 64 FX Athlon 64 X2 Athlon X2 Phenom FX Phenom X3 Phenom X4 Sempron	This motherboard supports a wide range of processors – but this time, they're all AMD processors.
Supported RAM	DDR2	Again, the industry standard.
Maximum RAM	8GB	This is pretty standard for motherboards and more than enough for even the most demanding user.
Supported RAM speeds	PC2-4300 PC2-6400 PC2-8500	Once again, when you're shopping for memory these are the numbers you need to know. Bigger means faster.
Integrated video	NVIDIA GeForce 8300	A pleasant surprise, this: the motherboard includes a good quality graphics card, although it uses system memory – so it's worth adding an extra 1GB to your memory plans.
Integrated audio	High Definition Audio	Once again you don't need a sound card, as the motherboard includes a high-quality, surround sound system.
Expansion slots	1 x PCI Express 16 1 x PCI Express x1 2 x PCI	We have our PCI Express 16 for graphics cards and PCI Express x1 and PCI for backwards compatibility, but this time there's no future-proof PCI 2.0 socket. It's not a huge issue, though: PCI Express 16 will be around for many years.
Storage interfaces	1 x ATA 5 x SATA 1 x eSATA	As with the previous motherboard we have a connector for older storage devices, one for external eSATA devices, and five SATA connectors for hard disks and DVD drives.
Other ports	12 x USB 1 x Gigabit Ethernet	No FireWire ports on this board, but that doesn't really matter as most devices use USB. You also get the standard single network port.

This time, we can see that we're looking for AMD processors, we don't need a sound card or a graphics card and we'll be able to stick our computer into a MicroATX case. The motherboard is reasonably future-proof – it has PCI Express 16; although it doesn't have PCI Express 2.0, that's unlikely to be a problem for a good few years – and it has plenty of connectors for SATA drives and USB ports. When we shop for RAM we need to look for PC2-4300, PC2-6400 or PC2-8500 DDR2 memory modules.

TECHIE CORNER

Chipset drivers You can't upgrade the chipset on an old motherboard but you can and should upgrade the chipset drivers periodically. Sometimes, motherboards are rushed to market and the software that controls the chipset – and hence the entire computer – doesn't work as it should. Sometimes it's downright broken. A driver update is often sufficient to bring the chipset up to speed and hence make the difference between a useful motherboard and a waste of money. Driver updates can also improve chipset performance in a key area such as integrated video. Pay occasional visits to the motherboard or chipset manufacturer's website and look for downloadable driver updates. We should also point out that the risk of running into driver and performance problems is significantly higher if you buy the very latest motherboard and/or chipset on the market, particularly when it's a motherboard manufacturer's first outing with that particular chipset. Why not let others have the headaches and plump for an almost-but-not-quite-spanking-new chipset where early teething troubles will have come to light and (hopefully) been remedied at source?

Intel, AMD and picking the perfect processor

As you've already spotted, Intel and its arch-rival AMD do things differently – so you can't put an AMD processor in a motherboard designed for Intel chips and vice versa. More importantly, you can't directly compare an Intel processor with an AMD one, because even if they have the same processor speeds the differences in the way they're made means you'd have more luck comparing apples and badgers. For example, when technology site Tom's Hardware compared Intel and AMD's processor ranges, it found that AMD's Phenom X4 9700 – a quad-core processor running at 2.4GHz – delivered almost identical performance to Intel's Core 2 Duo E6550, which is a dual-core processor running at 2.33GHz. However, that doesn't mean the Intel processor is faster: if software isn't designed to take advantage of multi-core processors, they won't be running at full power.

There's also money to consider. AMD processors can be pricier than the equivalent Intel ones, but AMD motherboards tend to be cheaper – and you'll often find (as we did when we built our small form factor PC) that an AMD processor–motherboard combination offers all the features you want at a much lower price than the Intel equivalent.

So which should you choose – Intel or AMD? The short answer is 'whichever you prefer'. While comparisons between Intel and AMD processors are largely meaningless, you can use the speeds to compare different processors from the same range – so you can expect a 2.66GHz processor to run slightly faster than a 2.4GHz one and considerably faster than a 1.8GHz one. We'd recommend setting a budget, seeing what Intel and AMD offer within your price bracket and then checking out a site, such as **www.extremetech.com**, to see how your shortlisted processors perform in real-world tests.

Chipset Conundrums

If you're considering an Intel-based PC, choosing a motherboard is straightforward enough: just find the right Intel chipset and everything follows from that. You'll find full details of Intel's chipset range at **www.intel.com/products/chipsets**. However, if you'd rather build an AMD-based system you'll need to delve a little deeper and find out what motherboards are available for your chosen processor.

That's something you should do anyway, because motherboards are not created equal. Different firms implement chipsets in different ways, so one firm might offer four PCI slots while another's otherwise identical motherboard offers six, or it might offer four USB ports while a rival firm's board gives you eight. There can be other differences too. Some motherboards supplement their audio connectors with digital outputs that you can connect to high-end audio equipment, while others have built-in wireless networking. Even within their own ranges, manufacturers have a seemingly endless list of motherboards based around a standard chipset but with each one offering slightly different connections or designs.

What that all means is that while it's important to choose the right chipset, unfortunately you'll still need to wade through different motherboards' specification sheets to make sure you're getting the one you really want. If you understand what the different specifications mean and have a clear idea of the kind of PC you want to build, picking the right motherboard is easy – and once you've chosen that, everything else falls swiftly into place.

For every Intel processor, there's an AMD alternative. This is the AMD Athlon 64 X2, a direct rival to dual-core Intel chips.

PART

Processor

The central processing unit – processor, or CPU, for short – is your PC's brain and its speed is a key factor in the overall performance of your PC. It's also a crucial marketing tool for manufacturers, who pack their ads with claims such as 'The fastest processor the world has ever seen!' or 'The processor's so fast, it'll do things before you've even decided to do them!' Of course, the ads have a point: when it comes to your new computer, you should get the fastest processor you can find. Shouldn't you?

Not necessarily. There are two very good reasons why you should ignore the very latest CPUs. The first is that they're far too expensive and the second is that you almost certainly don't need and won't benefit from them.

Let's say you want silky-smooth performance in absolutely everything. Intel's mighty Core 2 Extreme Quad QX9770, with four processors running at 3.2GHz, is bound to be a beauty – and it is, if you've got nearly a thousand pounds sitting around: at the time of writing, that particular processor costs £929.37. It's fast – Tom's Hardware tested it and it took just 102 seconds to render high-definition video footage, which is one of the most demanding things you can possibly ask a PC to do – but is it really £800 faster than the Core 2 Duo E7200, which took a perfectly respectable 282 seconds to do the same job and costs

Intel's Core Duo is the replacement for the Pentium processor and it has already evolved into the Core 2 Duo processor and the Core 2 Extreme processor.

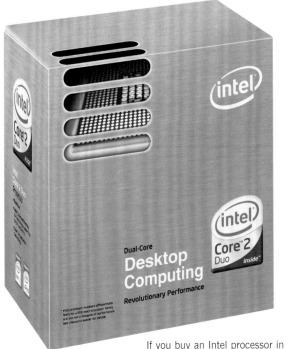

If you buy an Intel processor in retail packaging, the box also includes the processor heatsink and cooling fan. If you go for a cheaper OEM version, the heatsink isn't included.

just £86.36? On a more real-world task, converting music into MP3 digital music files using the iTunes program, the £929 processor took 64 seconds while the £86 one took 83 seconds. There's a difference, sure, but it's hardly dramatic.

The truth is that unless you're trying to make a computer-animated movie such as *Toy Story 2* in your back bedroom, a recent AMD Athlon or Intel Core 2 Duo will have more than enough horsepower for everyday tasks. A cutting-edge processor won't make you type any faster or make things download from the internet more quickly, so unless you're determined to make the fastest PC the world has ever seen there's no need to spend hundreds of pounds on a processor – especially if it leaves you so short of cash that you end up buying a slow hard disk, insufficient memory and an underpowered graphics card.

Processor evolution

The history of processors is long and duller than dishwater, so let's stick to the things you actually need to know. The table below shows recent Intel processors from the Pentium 4 onwards, together with the key features of those chips. Where the table shows more than one figure the lowest figure is for the earliest, slowest chips and the highest is for the latest, fastest ones.

Processor	Type	Clock speed[1] (GHz)	L2 Cache[2] (MB)	FSB (MHz)	Socket
Core i7	Quad core	2.66–3.06	8	QuickPath	LGA1366
Core 2 Extreme	Quad core	2.66–3.2	4–12	1066–1600	LGA771/775
Core 2 Duo	Dual core	1.8–2.67	2–4	800–1,066	Socket 775
Pentium D	Dual core	2.8–3.6	2–4	533–800	Socket 775
Pentium 4	Single core	1.3–3.8	.025–2	400–1,066	Socket 423/478/775

[1] Clock speed is a measure of a processor's work rate, expressed in millions (MHz) or billions (GHz) of cycles per second. The higher the clock speed, the more instructions the processor can carry out per second, although that's not the whole story: the FSB speed and other components, such as memory, also affect the processor's real-world performance. Remember too that clock speeds for dual-core systems are per core. Another issue to consider is that different processor architectures means that comparisons between different processor families aren't possible. For example, Core 2 Duo clock speeds are clearly lower than those of later Pentium 4s, but they don't have the Pentium 4's famously inefficient Netburst architecture. That means they need fewer instructions to do identical tasks and, as a result, they're much more efficient and run much more quickly. Similarly, you can't directly compare a Core 2 Extreme with a Core i7 processor as the latter uses a completely different architecture called QuickPath Interconnect, which is a replacement for the traditional front side bus (FSB) technology that's capable of delivering up to 25.6GB per second data transfer.

[2] Level 2 cache is a sliver of extremely fast memory that lives inside the processor and speeds up communication between the CPU and the chipset, so the more you have the merrier you will be. On some multi-core processors, the cache figures are per core.

As you can see, processors have evolved in three key areas: clock speed, cache size and FSB speeds. However, something else has happened too, which is that each processor line eventually reaches the limits of its underlying technology. The Pentium 4 hit the buffers at 3.8GHz, by which point the dual-core Pentium D had already appeared. The Pentium D took its place for a while but was supplanted by the more efficient and more powerful Core 2 Duo. It is still around, but its replacements are already on sale: the quad-core Core 2 Extreme and the even newer Core i7 processors which, according to the entirely unbiased Intel, are 'the best desktop processors on the planet'.

A similar evolution has taken place in AMD processors, with Athlons becoming Athlon XPs, Athlon 64s and dual-core Athlon 64 X2s, which in turn led to triple- and quad-core Phenom processors. As with Intel chips, over time AMD has boosted its processors' cache memory and evolved its motherboard socket designs, so the most recent AMD chips use the AM2+ socket design while older chips need Socket A motherboards.

Whether you go for an Intel or an AMD chip, it's worth bearing in mind that the faster processors in their ranges use more power and emit more heat than the slower ones, so they may require more powerful power supplies and better cooling systems than their cheaper, less powerful siblings.

In addition to the two firms' desktop processors, Intel and AMD both make mobile versions of their processors. These are primarily designed for laptops where battery life is more important than outright performance. Intel has the Pentium M and, today, the Core 2 Duo Mobile; AMD has the Sempron, the Mobile Athlon and the Turion range. Unless you're building an ultra-small PC where energy efficiency is your number one priority, you'll be better off with a dedicated desktop CPU. We'll look at mobile processors in more detail in a moment.

Two cores or not two cores?

Comparing processors used to be easy: a 2GHz chip was twice as fast as a 1GHz one. However, the current generation of processors boasts multi-core technology, which means that the chip manufacturer has crammed two, three or four CPUs onto a single chip. As if that wasn't enough, Intel reckons that we may be using 80-core CPUs by 2011. So what does this mean for the budding PC builder?

On paper, a dual-core system should be much faster than a single-core one. For example, a dual-core processor running at 1.67GHz should easily outperform a single-core processor that runs at 2.8GHz, and a triple- or quad-core processor at a similar speed should outperform the dual-core processor. And that's true, provided your software supports it. Windows XP, Windows Vista and Windows 7 support multi-core technology, but older versions of Windows don't and some games haven't caught up yet.

The main advantage of a multi-core processor is that it can do several things at once. Single-core chips only pretend to multitask, which is why your system often becomes sluggish if you're running two programs simultaneously. You'll notice a big difference between a single-core CPU and a dual-core one when you try to do something demanding while still using your PC; for example, if you're ripping CDs to Windows Media Player while writing an angry letter to the bank, running a full virus scan and downloading files from the internet, a dual-core system will be considerably smoother and more responsive. If you're only doing one demanding thing, such as rendering video, the CPU uses both of its brains at once.

For demanding tasks – editing really big digital photos, working with video, using your PC as a digital video recorder while simultaneously doing the accounts and digitising your record collection – we'd definitely recommend a multi-core processor. However, if money's tight and you don't really need to multitask it might be a better idea to get a really fast Pentium 4 and a motherboard that enables you to pop in a dual-core chip later on.

One of the best things that's happened since the last edition of this book is that processor prices have plummeted, so even recent dual-core chips are affordable: while the fastest multi-core chips are well over £600, dual-core Intel and AMD chips start at around £100. If you don't want or don't need dual-core processing, Pentium 4s are currently selling for around £40.

Celerons and Semprons

In addition to their main desktop processors, Intel and AMD also make low-powered chips that are particularly well-suited to laptops, budget computers and small form factor PCs. Such processors have different names to their desktop equivalents, so for example the cut-down Pentium chip is known as the Celeron and the cut-down Athlon is the Sempron.

There are two main differences between Celerons or Semprons and their mainstream equivalents. The first is price; for example, at the time of writing, **www.maplin.co.uk** is offering a fairly speedy Sempron 3400 and a motherboard for under £70. That's around the same price as a stand-alone Pentium 4 processor and roughly half the price of a Pentium 4 and motherboard. However, the second and most important difference is performance. Celerons and Semprons have been designed from the outset as low-cost processors and, in order to build chips to a budget, corners have to be cut somewhere.

To use a car analogy, let's say your PC is a Ford Focus. The Celeron and Sempron are the entry-level engines that appear in the cheapest Focuses; while they'll get you from A to B, they're not as swift, as smooth or as efficient as the more expensive engines available. Returning to the world of PCs, that's why the very cheapest PCs you'll see on sale are running Celerons while the ones targeted at power users have the latest Core 2 Duos or Athlon XP chips.

So where have corners been cut? Typically you'll find that such processors have smaller on-board cache memory and slower bus speeds than their big brothers; as a result, they don't offer the same blistering performance. It's not a huge issue for everyday computing, but if you plan to use your PC for demanding tasks such as video editing or cutting-edge gaming then you might find that the low-cost chips don't deliver the performance you need.

Another issue to consider is the processor's support for other bits of your PC. For example, AMD's site shows that its latest Semprons support the PC 3200 standard for memory, which runs at 667MHz. That's perfectly respectable and fine for the majority of applications, but it's not as fast as the newer PC 6400 standard with its 800MHz bus speed. If you want your homebrew PC to use the very latest and fastest memory technology, cut-down processors aren't the way to go.

If you're considering a Celeron or Sempron, the same issues apply as when you're shopping for a Core Duo or Athlon chip: different chips use different sockets and run at different bus speeds, so it's important to choose your motherboard and processor combination carefully to make sure they're a perfect match.

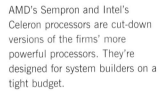

AMD's Sempron and Intel's Celeron processors are cut-down versions of the firms' more powerful processors. They're designed for system builders on a tight budget.

They come in many shapes and sizes but, stylish or otherwise, a heatsink is an essential accoutrement for a hot CPU.

Cooling

Processors get very, very hot when in use and need to be adequately cooled. This usually involves a heatsink unit with a built-in fan that attaches directly to the processor by means of clips. The heatsink has aluminium fins that dissipate heat generated by the hot core of the processor and the fan cools it with a constant flow of air. Many motherboards also have a secondary heatsink to cool the Northbridge chip.

Without a heatsink, a processor would soon overheat and either shut itself down, if you are lucky, or burn out completely and probably take the motherboard with it.

All retail processors ship with suitable units in the box. Indeed, this is one very good reason to pay a little more for the retail packaging. If you source an OEM processor – i.e. one originally supplied to a computer manufacturer and later resold – you will also have to buy a compatible heatsink/fan. This is no great problem but do be sure to get one rated for the clock speed of your processor. It must also be designed for the appropriate socket i.e. a Socket 775 heatsink won't fit in a Socket 478 motherboard.

We cover the installation of heatsinks in detail later. See also Appendix 1 on quiet PCs.

Memory

System memory – Random Access Memory (RAM) – is just as critical a component in your new computer as the processor. More so, even. Too little memory and the fastest processor in the world will choke on its workload; stacks of memory and you can run several software applications at the same time without the system stuttering, hanging or crashing.

At the simplest level, computer applications run in RAM, by which we mean the files required to open and maintain a given program are transferred from the hard disk, where the program is installed, to RAM for the duration of the session. If you turn off your computer or it crashes, RAM's memory is 'flushed' or wiped out, so you have to start again. That's why it's so very important to save your work as you go along. Only then are your changes copied from RAM back to the hard drive for permanent storage.

Let's say you want to perform a sum in a spreadsheet. The spreadsheet program isolates the data required to perform the sum. RAM then sends this data to the processor through the Front Side Bus (or in the case of an Athlon 64 processor, directly via the integrated memory controller). The processor crunches the numbers, comes up with an answer, and sends it back to RAM. Finally, RAM feeds the result to your spreadsheet program and the solution appears on your monitor screen.

It all happens very quickly indeed. However, in all but the most intensive applications, such as real-time video editing, the overall speed of the system is governed far more by RAM than by the processor. When a computer runs painfully slowly, chances are that RAM is the bottleneck, not the processor.

Some memory modules sport their very own heatsinks to help diffuse the heat. Cynics argue that these bolt-on accessories are mainly for show, like go-faster stripes.

How much memory do I really need?

Windows supports up to 4MB of RAM if you install a 32-bit version, although for reasons far too dull to go into here you'll only actually get 3.5MB of usable memory – check out

www.codinghorror.com/blog/archives/000811.html if you'd like to know why – but 64-bit Windows Vista and Windows 7 support as much memory as you can throw at them. We'd recommend 2GB of RAM, double that if you're planning to play cutting-edge games, work with enormous digital images or experiment with video editing.

If you'll be using lots of programs simultaneously, remember that system requirements are usually per program, so while Microsoft Office 2007 says it needs 256MB of RAM that is over and above the memory that Windows needs to function.

It's also worth reading the small print, because there can be nasty surprises lurking. For example, if you dig around the system requirements of Office 2007 and look at the footnotes, you'll discover that while Office asks for 256MB of RAM you need 512MB for Outlook 2007's Instant Search feature. You'll also discover that Word 2007's real-time grammar and spelling checker won't even switch on if your PC has less than 1GB of installed RAM.

If your PC has integrated graphics, you'll need to factor that in too: integrated graphics systems grab some of your PC's system RAM as they don't have their own memory chips. Depending on how you configure your system that means your video card will take 256MB, 512MB or even 1GB of RAM, which of course reduces the amount of memory available to Windows and your various programs.

Modules

RAM comes in the form of chips soldered to long, thin modules that plug into slots on the motherboard. These modules are remarkably easy to install but buying the right modules in the first place is a more complicated matter.

As mentioned above, any motherboard/chipset supports one type of RAM and one alone. This is not to say that you should buy your motherboard first and then look for compatible memory modules as an afterthought. Quite the reverse, in fact: as soon as you've decided between an Intel or an AMD processor, turn your thoughts to RAM and let this decision govern your choice of chipset (and hence motherboard).

Now, we could fill the rest of this manual with techie talk about memory evolution, error-checking, voltages, transistor counts, latency and so forth, but it would make your eyes glaze over and get us almost nowhere. Let's focus instead on the absolute essentials.

DDR-RAM

Memory chips have come in a variety of standards over the years: SD-RAM, RD-RAM, DDR, DDR2 and DDR3. Unless you're planning to use a fairly old motherboard – and when you consider how cheap modern motherboards are, that's probably a false economy – then the one you need to know about is DDR2. DDR2 stands for Dual Double Data Rate RAM and it comes in modules known as Double Inline Memory Modules – DIMMs for short.

So what does all this dual double rate stuff actually mean? Before DDR RAM came along, memory transferred data according to your motherboard's clock speed, so if your clock speed was 200MHz your memory would be capable of transferring data 200 million times per second. With Dual Data Rate RAM (DDR), however, the memory could send and receive data twice per clock cycle – so in the case of our 200MHz clock speed, it would be transferring data 400 times per second. DDR2 takes things a step further and transfers data at four times the clock speed, so to use our 200MHz clock once again we'd be transferring data 800 times per second. The recent DDR3 standard ups the stakes again and shuffles data around at eight times the clock speed, and no doubt there will be a DDR4 standard that doubles that.

At the time of writing, DDR2 is the one you need to know

There are 184 pins in this DDR DIMM. DDR memory is compatible with both Intel and AMD processors.

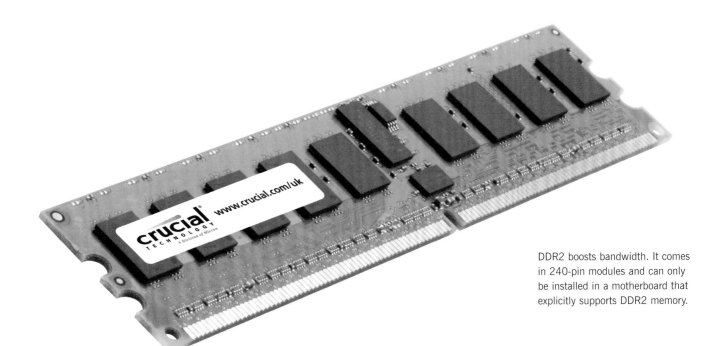

DDR2 boosts bandwidth. It comes in 240-pin modules and can only be installed in a motherboard that explicitly supports DDR2 memory.

about: while motherboards are beginning to support DDR3 memory modules, they're massively outnumbered by DDR2-supporting motherboards. For now DDR3 is more expensive and harder to find than DDR2 and there's little point in even considering it unless you're going for the fastest, most recent and most expensive processors. Until DDR3 rules the roost, which will take a good few years, DDR2 is almost certainly the kind of memory you'll be putting into your system.

Dual-channel memory

Many motherboards support dual-channel memory configurations. The idea is that you can run two modules in parallel at the same time to effectively double the bandwidth between RAM and the processor, which speeds up your system. The trick is having two memory controllers on the motherboard.

The standard analogy for dual-channel memory is a jammed motorway. Let's say you have three lanes of traffic cruising at 70mph. If you want to get more cars from A to B in a given time, what can you do? Well, first you can increase the traffic flow by raising the speed limit. This is akin to running memory at ever-faster clock speeds. So now you have a three-lane motorway with traffic hurtling along at 140mph. The next option is squeezing more cars into the available space. This is DDR2's approach. Traffic moves at the same speed – 70mph – but now there's twice as much of it. However, the motorway is now running at full speed with no spare room (or safe distance) between the vehicles. What else can you do to shift more traffic?

You can build an identical motorway alongside the first. This is what a dual-channel memory configuration does. Apply the methodology to a motherboard and in theory it shifts twice as much data to the processor and thus does everything twice as quickly. In practice, the benefits are more modest but it's still an increased performance that you can feel rather than merely chart in a benchmark test.

SD-RAM Before DDR2, DDR and RD-RAM, we had humble Synchronous Dynamic RAM. SD-RAM is dynamic because its contents are flushed continually and lost altogether when you turn off your computer; and it's synchronous because it is synchronised for performance with the motherboard's memory bus. DDR and DDR2 are merely enhancements of this original standard.

Presumably there are still motherboards around that support SD-RAM but only on the second-hand market. Suitable memory modules are also very difficult to obtain. Memory is a commodity market where demand drives supply and there's simply no call for fresh SD-RAM these days. However, it looks likely that DDR will gradually be superseded by DDR2 so, even if you are on an extremely tight budget, we'd strongly advise you to forget about defunct SD-RAM and hang on for a DDR bargain. As with every development in computer generations, the previous, still-powerful generation gets marked down in price very, very quickly. This means that high-bandwidth, high-capacity DDR memory modules will soon be cheap as chips.

You can still get hold of SD-RAM for older motherboards but it's not exactly flying out of Taiwan's fabrication plants these days.

The critical thing about dual-channelling is that you must use two identical modules and install them in the correct slots. If you try to dual-channel with modules of different speeds or capacities, it will not work.

We'll leave the last word to the respected computing site Tom's Hardware, which tested single- and dual-channel DDR2 memory:

The performance difference between single channel and dual channel DDR2-800 memory using an up-to-date Core 2 Duo system is little to nil. Most tests show differences, but they are really small. For games and enthusiast PCs, we recommend sticking to high-performance dual channel RAM, because the memory is one of those components that you want to perform best for a smooth experience. For regular applications, though, it doesn't really matter much whether you run single or dual channel.

Here's a summary of the current possibilities with DDR, DDR2 and DDR3 memory modules:

Memory name	Internal clock speed (MHz)	Data transfers per cycle	External memory bus speed (MHz)	Bus width (bits)	Bandwidth (MB/sec)
PC1600 DDR-200	100	2	200	64	1,600
PC2100 DDR-266	133	2	266	64	2,100
PC2700 DDR-333	167	2	333	64	2,700
PC 3200 DDR-400	200	2	400	64	3,200
PC3700 DDR-466	233	2	466	64	3,700
PC4000 DDR-500	250	2	500	64	4,000
PC4300 DDR-533	266	2	533	64	4,300
PC2-3200 DDR2-400	100	4	200	64	3,200
PC2-4200 DDR2-533	133	4	266	64	4,200
PC2-5300 DDR2-667	166	4	333	64	5,300
PC2-6400 DDR2-800	200	4	400	64	6,400
PC2-8500 DDR2-1066	266	4	533	64	8,533
PC3-6400 DDR3-800	100	8	400	64	6,400
PC3-8500 DDR3-1066	133	8	533	64	8,533
PC3-10600 DDR3-1333	166	8	667	64	10,667
PC3-12800 DDR3-1600	200	8	800	64	12,800

Selecting memory

The first rule when buying memory is to get the fastest sort that the motherboard supports. That is, if your motherboard chipset supports both 400 and 533MHz buses, spend that little extra on DDR or DDR2 533 modules. If it also supports dual-channel, buy matching pairs and install them in the appropriate slots (see p.84–5). In fact, we highly recommend that you consider only dual-channel motherboards if you want peak performance. Remember, dual-channel uses standard DDR or DDR2 modules so you effectively get twice the performance for no extra outlay. If you take the DDR2 route, consider buying more expensive low-latency modules for an extra boost.

Here's another recommendation: don't attempt to match memory modules to motherboards yourself. It's a truly fraught process so make it easy on yourself with an online memory configuration tool. With these, you enter motherboard details at one end and at the other end out pops a list of compatible modules.

Let's jump the gun and test one out.

*Crucial Technology's Memory Adviser (**www.crucial.com/uk**) invites you to tell it who made your computer, which isn't a very promising start for a DIY system builder. What it really needs to know, of course, are the motherboard details. If you have a motherboard in mind or if you have already bought one, select the manufacturer here. In this example, it is Gigabyte. In the next couple of steps, select your precise model. Choose carefully.*

The screen also gives you frequently asked questions, such as whether your motherboard supports dual-channel memory. In this case the answer is 'Yes'. The Memory Adviser helpfully presents a summary of your chosen motherboard's memory support. It's well worth double-checking this against the official specification. Here, for instance, we learn that the motherboard supports up to 4GB (or 4,096MB, which is the same thing) of DDR2 memory in either the PC3200 or PC4300 flavours (a.k.a. DDR2-400 and DDR2-533) in a 240-pin DIMM format.
(What Crucial refers to as PC2 4200 appears in our table on p.42 as PC4300. The terms are interchangeable. The additional '2' in PC2 is also optional.)

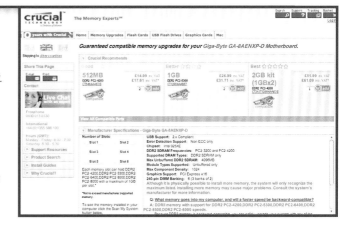

At the top of the screen you'll see three memory deals, but if you scroll down there are lots of other memory modules. Choose carefully: this motherboard only supports up to PC4300 memory, so buying the first item – PC8000 – is a waste of money, because it will run at PC4300 speeds. The same applies to option 2 at the top of the screen – it's faster than the motherboard can actually handle. It pays to check these things very carefully when you're on a budget.

PART  Case

Just as all motherboards adhere to certain industry-standard dimensions, so too do computer cases. Far and away the most common form factor is, again, ATX. You can be sure that any ATX motherboard will fit in any ATX case. That's the kind of simplicity that we appreciate. But that's not to say that all cases are the same.

Towers vs desktops

Far from it, in fact. For starters, you can choose between a tower case or a desktop case. One is tall and narrow, the other squat and wide. We heartily recommend going for a tower case. They are overwhelmingly more prevalent than desktop cases and, in our experience, considerably easier to work with. The exception would be if you're building a home-entertainment-style PC for living room use. In this case, style matters almost as much as function.

You can get full-sized, mid-sized and mini tower cases, which are progressively shorter versions of the same thing. The sole advantage of a low-rise tower is neatness; the considerable disadvantage is a corresponding lack of expansion possibilities. A mini-tower will typically have two or three 5.25-inch drive bays, a mid-tower between three and five, and a full-tower anywhere up to seven. Given that you will probably install a CD-RW drive and a DVD-ROM drive, a three-bay case still has room for one

Here we see a full tower case with a side panel removed and its front fascia on and off.

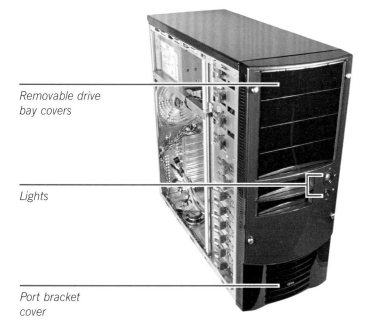

Removable drive bay covers

Lights

Port bracket cover

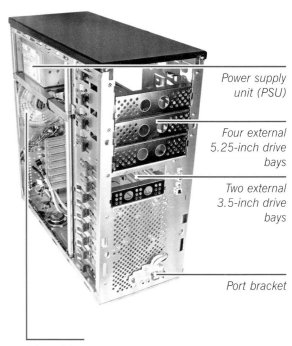

Power supply unit (PSU)

Four external 5.25-inch drive bays

Two external 3.5-inch drive bays

Port bracket

Internal fan

Aluminium cases like this one from Lian-Li are light, strong and cool.

additional device (a sound card breakout box, perhaps) whereas a two-bay case would effectively be full.

Pay attention to 3.5-inch drive bays, too. You'll need at least one for the hard disk drive and another for the floppy drive/card reader. However, we're going to recommend that you install two hard drives and possibly as many as four. Spare internal drive bays thus rank somewhere between desirable and essential.

In short, you want to allow your PC room to grow. Of course, it's always possible to strip the entire innards from a computer and reinstall everything in a larger case should the need arise, but this is about the most drastic and fiddly upgrade you could ever perform. Better, we suggest, to allow for future expansion at the outset.

A non-ATX small form factor platform like this offers little in the way of expansion possibilities, but you may consider that a fair compromise if you need a looker for the living room.

Case features

Drive bays are protected by drive bay covers on the front of the case. These snap-out or unscrew to afford full access to the bay, whereupon you can install an internally-mounted drive.

A case also has a series of blanking plates to the rear that correspond to the motherboard's expansion slots. You'll remove one every time you install an expansion card. Above this is a rectangular input-output (I/O) panel. This is where the mouse, keyboard, parallel, serial and other ports poke through when the motherboard is installed.

On the front of the case, you will find two buttons: the main power on/off switch and a smaller, usually recessed reset button that restarts your computer if Windows hangs. There will be a couple of lights, too: one to show when the power is on and one that flickers whenever the hard disk drive is particularly active. The case may also have an extra opening to accommodate an expansion bracket loaded with audio or USB ports.

Your case may have a single all-encompassing cover that lifts straight off or separate removable side panels. It may be held together with screws, thumbscrews or some arrangement of clips. Internally, you may find a removable motherboard tray. This is a boon, as it's much easier to install the motherboard on an external tray than it is to fiddle around inside the case.

Inside the case, along with the drive bays and a cluster of cables, you'll find a pre-installed fan or two and possibly a mounting area for an optional extra fan. The case will also have a speaker which the BIOS will use to generate beeps (see p.160).

Beyond all of this, designs vary from the standard, boring 'big beige box' look to undeniably funky. Pressed-steel cases are generally cheaper but brushed-aluminium looks (and stays) cooler. Some cases are heavy, reinforced and thoroughly sturdy; others are lightweight, flimsy and easily dented. We would simply advise you to focus on functionality before frills. A full-sized tower case is generally easier to work with, easier to keep tidy internally, more adaptable to customisation and provides better airflow to the motherboard's components.

The same case we saw a moment ago, stripped of its covers and seen from the rear.

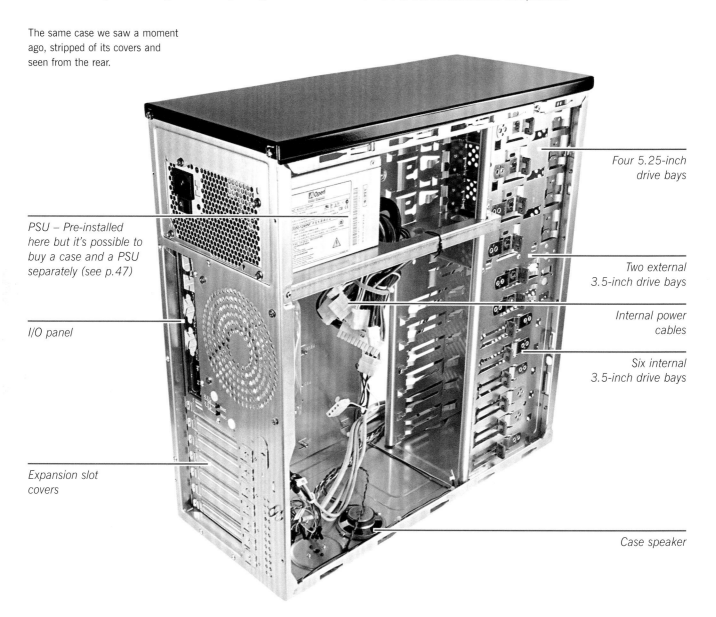

Four 5.25-inch drive bays

PSU – Pre-installed here but it's possible to buy a case and a PSU separately (see p.47)

Two external 3.5-inch drive bays

Internal power cables

I/O panel

Six internal 3.5-inch drive bays

Expansion slot covers

Case speaker

PART  Power supply unit

The power supply unit (PSU) supplies power to the computer's motherboard and drives. That much is obvious. Less so is the importance of getting the right PSU, particularly when many cases come with an anonymous unit pre-installed. Ignore the specifications here and you risk all sorts of problems. If possible, purchase your case and PSU separately, or at least devote as much care to the PSU as to every other component.

Compatibility

A reliable power supply unit is a must. This ATX model has an adjustable fan speed for quiet running and pumps out 350W.

To go with your ATX case and ATX motherboard, you need an ATX PSU. Virtually all new PSUs comply with the ATX standard, which means it will fit in an ATX case and power an ATX motherboard.

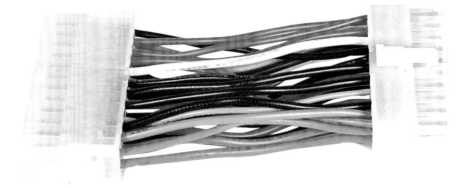

An adapter for converting a 24-pin PSU connector to a 20-pin motherboard.

However, if you are using an Intel processor and a Socket 775 motherboard, take care. You'll need one of the newer PSUs that has a 24-pin power connector rather than the older 20-pin standard. If you intend to reuse an older PSU or if you buy a 20-pin unit and later find that you can't connect it to your motherboard, all is not lost: you can buy an adapter to convert a 20-pin connector to a 24-pin connector. However, this is not advisable unless the PSU pumps out at least 450W of power. We strongly recommend that you buy a new 24-pin PSU instead. Conversely, though, you can also get an adapter to convert a new 24-pin PSU for use with an older 20-pin motherboard, and that's risk-free.

Also ensure that you get a PSU with SATA connectors if you have a SATA-enabled motherboard and SATA hard drives. Again, an adapter or two can save the day but it is better to buy the appropriate equipment in the first place.

We don't recommend buying a second-hand PSU. An under-powered PSU might not supply power-hungry components with the juice they need, particularly if you cram your case full of drives and accessories, and an older unit with a history of hard work behind it is obviously more liable to burn out and die.

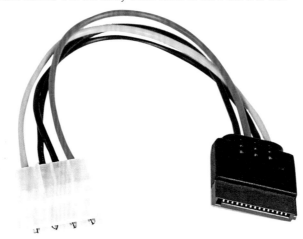

An IDE-to-SATA adapter for powering new-style drives from an older PSU.

Yet another adapter. This one converts a Molex cable into a pair of SATA connectors.

Power rating

A 250W or 300W PSU is inadequate, 350W is fine and 400W is better still. Simple as that.

Cooling

A PSU has an integrated fan that controls airflow through the computer case. Some also have a second fan that blows cool air at the motherboard. We strongly recommend that you buy a PSU specifically rated for the kind of processor you intend to use.

Noise

A secondary consideration, certainly, but important nonetheless. Some PSUs make a terrible racket while others operate with barely a whisper. If a peaceful PC is important to you, shop around for a quiet device with adjustable-speed fans. See also Appendix 1.

Connectors

The PSU connects directly to each internal drive in your PC and to the motherboard itself, supplying the lot with power. Here's a run through of what to expect.

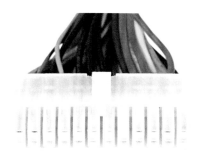

ATX power The main power connector that plugs directly into the motherboard. As mentioned above, the design has switched recently from 20-pin plugs to 24-pin.

ATX Auxiliary A secondary 6-pin power connection required by some older motherboards. If your motherboard has an ATX Auxiliary socket, you must connect this cable.

ATX 12V Some Pentium 4 motherboards require yet another cable connection from the PSU to provide extra power to the processor. However, the latest Socket 775 motherboards dispense with this.

Molex drive connector Used to power hard disk and optical drives.

SATA drive connector Used to power Serial ATA hard drives (and some of the latest optical drives).

Berg drive connector Used primarily to power the floppy drive.

Hard disk drive

In recent years, hard disks have grown dramatically in size – which is just as well, because the amount of storage space the average PC user needs has increased dramatically too. Digital media – that is, photos, music and video – are the worst offenders; for example, if you're using a high-definition video camcorder, a two-minute clip takes around 200MB of space. That's a fifth of a gigabyte!

You can of course add extra storage later – if your PC has a spare USB port you can easily connect an external hard disk – but it's cheaper to buy a bigger hard disk when you build your PC than to skimp on storage now and have to buy more in the not-too-distant future. The good news is that hard disks with capacities of 500GB or more have plummeted in price and they're cheap enough to consider for your home-made PC project.

A hard disk drive stores data on high-speed spinning magnetic platters. Remarkably, they last for tens of thousands of hours.

Interface

There's more to a hard disk than its size: its interface is important too. You can't connect a SATA drive to a motherboard that only supports IDE or vice versa and that means you need to know about the different interface options.

Until recently, the two most common hard disk interfaces were IDE (Integrated Drive Electronics, sometimes prefixed with an extra E for Enhanced) and ATA (Advanced Technology Attachment). Although technically distinct, these terms are used interchangeably to describe the connection between the hard disk drive and the motherboard. However, while most modern motherboards still support these standards, they're much keener on the newer Serial ATA (SATA) standard, which is faster and simpler than its predecessors – and it uses thinner, smaller cables, which makes it tidier and better for air circulation too. More often than not, when you buy a motherboard it will have a single ATA/IDE interface and several SATA ones.

Interface	Also known as	Maximum bandwidth (MB/sec)
ATA-66	ATA-5, IDE-66 or UDMA-66	66
ATA-100	ATA-6, IDE-100 or UDMA-100	100
ATA-133	ATA-7, IDE-133 or UDMA-133	133
SATA-150	SATA I	150
SATA-300	SATA II	300

Data transfer rates

The real-world performance of a drive doesn't just depend on the bandwidth. In fact, many an ATA-100 drive can outpace an ATA-133 device at reading or saving large files. It comes down to a specification called the internal, or sustained, transfer rate. This is a measure of how quickly a drive can read data from its own disks. The bandwidth figures quoted above relate to the external transfer rate but this merely tells you how quickly the drive can shift data out to the main system. Manufacturers are notoriously reticent about sustained transfer rates, one reason being that the figure is significantly lower than the headline-grabbing external interface.

Sustained transfer rates peak between around 40–70MB/sec, which is some way short of even the ATA-100 standard's external transfer rate, let alone SATA's 150MB/sec and up. The drive may be perfectly capable of pumping out huge volumes of data but this is of questionable value if it can't gather this data at anything like the same rate. The bottleneck is the drive itself, not the interface.

Cables

For an ATA-66 or faster HDD, use only an 80-conductor IDE/ATA cable. This has the same plugs as the older 40-conductor style and looks very similar, but it incorporates twice as many wires within the ribbon. The extra wires are essentially non-functional, but they reduce interference and help preserve a true signal.

Two drives sharing an IDE/ATA channel on the motherboard must be allocated master and slave status in order that the motherboard can tell them apart. This is achieved with little plastic jumpers on the drives. If you mistakenly set both drives to Master or to Slave, neither will work. However, with an 80-conductor cable you can set all drives to the Cable Select position and forget about them: the cable sorts out master/slave status automatically.

With SATA, it's simpler still. This is a one-drive-per-channel technology, which means no more sharing, no more master/slave status, and no more jumpers.

A 40-conductor IDE/ATA cable, an 80-conductor IDE/ATA cable, and a SATA cable.

TECHIE CORNER

As an alternative to IDE/ATA or Serial ATA, you might consider SCSI (Small Computer Systems Interface). This is a high-speed interface suited to all manner of drives and devices, from scanners and external CD drives to internal hard disk drives. The main advantage is one of performance: a SCSI drive is usually faster than an IDE/ATA drive, with data transfer rates across the bus of up to 160 or 320MB/sec (Ultra160 and Ultra320 respectively). Again, however, the interface speed is largely theoretical; the drive's real-world performance depends more upon its sustained transfer rate, and this will not necessarily be faster than an IDE/ATA drive. Moreover, gigabyte for gigabyte, SCSI drives are very much more expensive than IDE/ATA devices. We can't, in all honesty, claim that the extra expense pays significant dividends.

Other considerations

Cache A slice of memory built into the drive that holds frequently accessed data in a buffer state. This saves the drive having to continually re-read from its disks. A 2MB cache is a good minimum; 8MB is desirable.

Spindle speed The rate at which the drive's disks spin. This has a bearing on how quickly the device can read and write data. 5,400rpm is adequate for a low-specification system but we'd recommend a 7,200rpm drive. As a not-entirely-consistent rule, a 7,200rpm drive will have a faster sustained transfer rate than a 5,400rpm drive.

S.M.A.R.T. An error-checking procedure that tries to predict when a hard disk drive is about to fail or, at least, has an increased risk of doing so. This gives you time to make a critical data backup. You need two things: a S.M.A.R.T.-enabled drive and either a motherboard BIOS with native support for S.M.A.R.T. or a standalone software program that works in tandem with the drive.

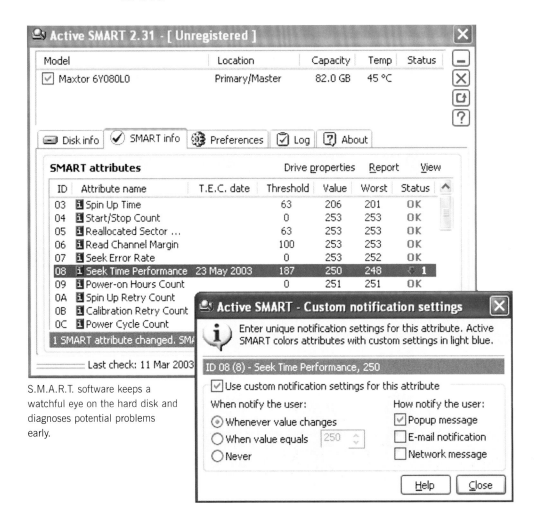

S.M.A.R.T. software keeps a watchful eye on the hard disk and diagnoses potential problems early.

RAID

Once the preserve of network servers, a RAID (Redundant Array of Independent Disks) setup is now a possibility for many home/office computers. Essentially, a RAID-supporting motherboard lets you use two or more hard disk drives simultaneously to 'stripe' or 'mirror' data.

With striping, also called RAID Level 0, the computer treats each hard disk as part of a whole. Two 60GB drives, for example, effectively become a single 120GB drive. Data is then distributed evenly between the drives, resulting in faster read/write performance. The risk is that a single drive failure means all data is lost.

With mirroring, or RAID Level 1, every file you save to the primary hard disk is simultaneously copied to every other drive in the system. Such duplication offers a high level of data security and reliability but, because the additional drives simply mirror the contents of the primary drive, you don't get the benefits of additional storage capacity. It's an expensive way to safeguard your files.

If you reckon RAID is for you, look for a chipset/motherboard with RAID drive controllers and RAID-compatible BIOS. Some motherboards support striping and mirroring simultaneously (Level 0+1), although for this you would need a grand total of four drives.

A RAID adapter expansion card provides additional sockets for connecting hard disks. This is a SATA model. However, an ever-increasing number of motherboards have built-in support for RAID and provide all the sockets you need.

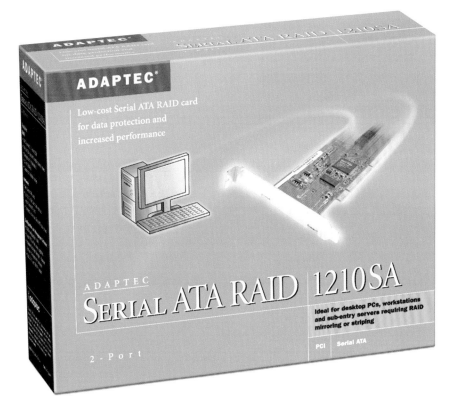

PART 4 Sound card

Before buying a sound card, ask yourself four questions:

Do you want to play music on your computer?

Do you want to play games on your computer?

Do you want to watch movies on your computer?

Do you want to record music on your computer?

The answers determine what kind of sound card you need.

A sound card such as Creative Labs Audigy 4 has more bells and whistles built into it than many an entire computer of yesteryear, and even comes with an external input/output box and a remote control. Essential equipment for the musician or gamer but only true audiophiles get really worked up about the nuances of one sound technology over another.

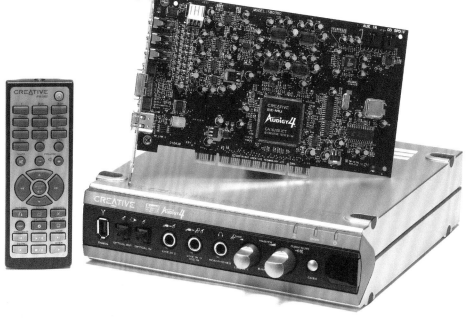

Music

For music playback, be it audio CD tracks, MP3 files or any other format, stereo is usually sufficient. Most music even today is still recorded in stereo so adding a few extra speakers here and there doesn't actually enhance it. That said, some audio hardware and/or software can 'upmix' a stereo signal to give an illusion of surround sound.

Games

Here you'll benefit from a multi-channel surround sound (or 'positional audio') system. This is where the audio signal is composed of several discrete channels relayed to satellite speakers strategically positioned around the listener.

The sound card should also support one or more of the popular sound technologies, including DirectSound3D, THX, A3D and EAX. The trouble is – as you will know if you've ever given this field more than a cursory glance – that there are so many competing, evolving and incompatible standards out there that it's simply impossible to get a sound card that supports everything and to keep up! Still, just about every game will play in a fall-back DirectX mode and should even install the requisite software for you.

Movies

DVD movie soundtracks are almost always encoded in 5.1 or 7.1 surround sound with Dolby Digital or DTS technology. This means you need five or seven satellite speakers plus a subwoofer (for low-frequency tones) to hear the full effect. You also need a sound card that can either decode the signal itself or pass it through to a separate decoder unit that sits between the card and the speakers.

Recording

Should you wish to connect a MIDI keyboard or other controller to your computer, you'll need a MIDI input. This is pretty much standard; most sound cards provide a combined MIDI/games controller port. Look for ASIO support, too. This is a driver standard that reduces the delay, or latency, between, for example, pressing a key on a MIDI keyboard and the sound registering with the recording software. Latency used to make multi-track recording a real pain but ASIO drivers help enormously.

Integrated versus expansion card

Before you start researching the world of sound cards, it's worth asking whether you need to buy one at all. Many motherboards provide very good integrated sound cards that deliver high-quality,

Fancy a cinema in your sitting room? Then you'll need a multi-channel sound system with speakers to do it justice.

QUICK Q&A

I picked up this old sound card from a stall but it doesn't fit in my PC!
That will be because you were sold an obsolete ISA card and your motherboard has only PCI expansion slots, as is the norm these days. See if you can exchange it for a PCI card.

surround-sound audio. There are two key standards to watch for here: AC'97 and the newer High Definition Audio standard. Both sound superb and, unless you're a musician or amazingly picky about sound quality, there's no real need to look any further.

The traditional disadvantage with integrated audio is that you only get a limited number of inputs and outputs – typically a few on the motherboard's I/O panel and perhaps an optional port bracket – and you may have to fiddle with software settings in order to connect the full array of speakers. However, we have seen more and more motherboard manufacturers wising up to these shortcomings and providing a full array of audio connectors on the I/O panel. Dropping outmoded interfaces like the parallel and serial ports helps to free up space.

In any event, we suggest that you select a motherboard with integrated audio and see how it suits. If you decide that you need a separate sound card after all, it's an easy upgrade to perform. Expansion cards always use the PCI interface these days. PCI Express versions will be along shortly but don't be fooled into thinking you need one: sound cards require very little bandwidth so there's no reason whatsoever to splash out on PCI Express when PCI is more than adequate.

When space is tight, sound ports typically double up duties. Two of the three ports here (lower right corner) function either as speaker outputs or as line and mic inputs, depending upon how the audio driver software is currently configured.

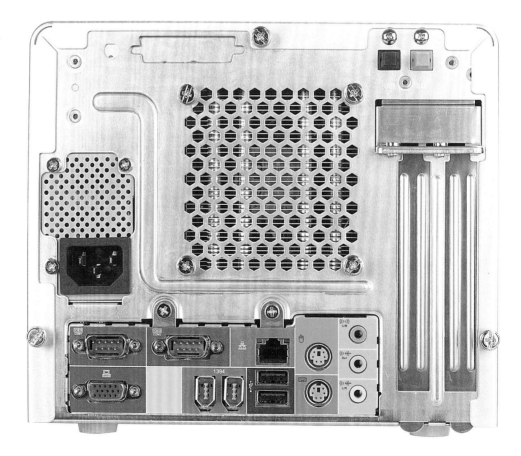

PART **2**

Video card

Like sound technology, the computer graphics arena is a fast-moving, ever-shifting, highly-competitive minefield of acronyms, abbreviations and indecipherable, incompatible 'standards'. Still, on we go ...

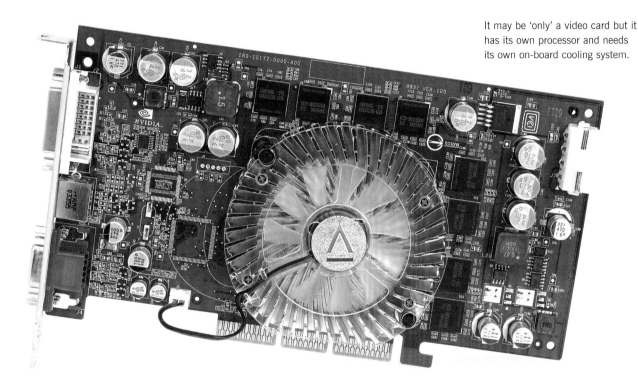

It may be 'only' a video card but it has its own processor and needs its own on-board cooling system.

QUICK Q&A

I've just been reading up on computer game standards and now my head hurts. What should I do?

Buy a PlayStation2? Sorry to sound flippant but computer gaming gives us a headache too. With a games console, you know that any game designed for that particular platform – PlayStation, Xbox, GameCube or whatever – will work straight out of the box with no configuration. Which is not to say that we are anti-computer gaming; it's just that we prefer the simplicity of a dedicated gaming platform, just as we'd rather watch a DVD movie on a television screen than a monitor.

Chipsets

Just as a motherboard is built around a chipset, so a video card (or graphics card, as they are also called) has at its heart a graphics processing unit (GPU). This is supported by a hefty slice of dedicated RAM located on the card itself. In effect, the video card is like a mini-computer in its own right, albeit with the very specific task of generating images on a monitor screen.

The two main GPU players right now are NVIDIA and ATI. Keep an eye on the latest Matrox cards, too, especially if you need multiple monitor support (see Quick Q&A on p.59).

2D/3D

It only takes 4MB of video memory to display a basic, two dimensional screen at 1024 x 768 pixels – but modern user interfaces, websites and programs use lots of colours, shadows and special effects, so you'll need a graphics card with considerably more than 4MB of RAM. Windows Vista and Windows 7 need at least 128MB of video memory to display properly – and 3D games need even more. Most video cards now have 512MB or even 1GB of RAM.

3D isn't really three-dimensional, of course, but the card uses complex lighting and texture techniques to create a realistic illusion of depth.

Interface

As we saw earlier, AGP (Accelerated Graphics Port) is a special slot on the motherboard reserved for video cards. At 266MB/sec, the single-speed version has double the bandwidth of PCI; at 8x-speed, it tops 2GB/sec. However, the AGP interface is now rapidly being replaced by PCI Express running at 16x-speed. This provides a massive 8GB/sec of bandwidth, which promises to prove a real (not just a theoretical) advantage for playing fast 3D computer games.

But PCI Express cards don't yet come cheap. Some motherboards have both AGP and PCI Express 16x-speed slots, in which case you can take your pick.

We said earlier that we are reluctant to recommend integrated video unless the motherboard also has a free expansion slot and we reiterate that now. It simply doesn't make sense to rule out future upgrades from the outset. However, if you are sure that 3D isn't your thing, or the children's, or the grandchildren's, a motherboard with an integrated video chip is certainly an economical purchase.

Sitting proudly in its PCI Express slot, this video card boasts up to 8GB of bandwidth – and a truly bizarre cooling system.

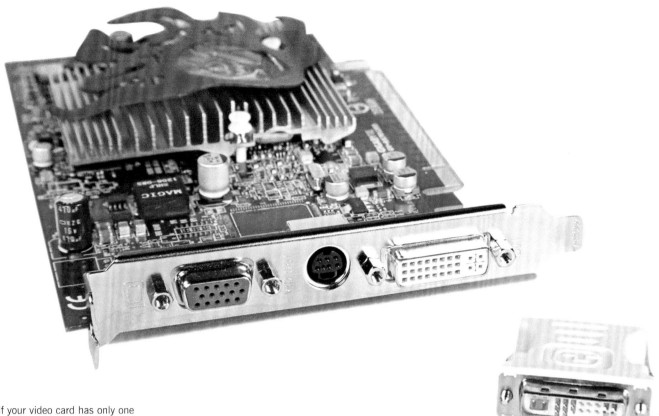

If your video card has only one
port, make sure that it's DVI.
This one also has VGA, which is
handy, but the alternative is a
DVI-to-VGA adapter.

DVI

A video card is a natively digital device that has to perform a
digital-to-analogue conversion in order to send a signal that an
analogue monitor can understand and display. This conversion
degrades the integrity of the signal to a degree (a small degree,
admittedly). Worse, modern flat-panel TFT monitors are actually
digital devices at heart so the analogue signal has to be re-
converted back to digital upon receipt. This is patently crazy,
hence the evolution of a purely digital connection between video
card and monitor: DVI (Digital Visual Interface).

When you connect a DVI monitor to a DVI video card, the
digital signal is transferred from one to the other more or less
wholesale. The result is a truer image with more faithful colour
representations. Better still, there's no need to mess around with
fiddly monitor controls in pursuit of a perfect picture: the card
and monitor work in harmony to display the best possible image
automatically.

The traditional 15-pin VGA plug and socket are disappearing
favour of DVI so a DVI-capable video card is a sensible purchase
If you have an analogue monitor with a VGA cable, a simple
adapter will get it connected until such time as you upgrade to
digital display.

? QUICK Q&A

**My video card has both VGA and DVI ports. Can I connect two
monitors?**

Probably not. Many video cards provide two outputs but these are mere
alternatives i.e. you can use one port or the other but not both
simultaneously. If you want to run two monitors, the usual approach is to
install a PCI video card alongside the AGP card and connect one monitor to
each. Windows recognises this arrangement automatically so configuration
is straightforward.

However, you can also get 'dual-head' and 'triple-head' video cards that
incorporate all the circuitry required to run two or three monitors through
the same bus. This is actually preferable because you get an AGP-generated
display on each monitor and it doesn't eat into your allocation of PCI slots.

For the best results with multiple-monitor displays, invest in a
specialist card like the Matrox Parhelia. One DVI channel can be
split to run two monitors, meaning that up to three can be
powered simultaneously from a single AGP interface.

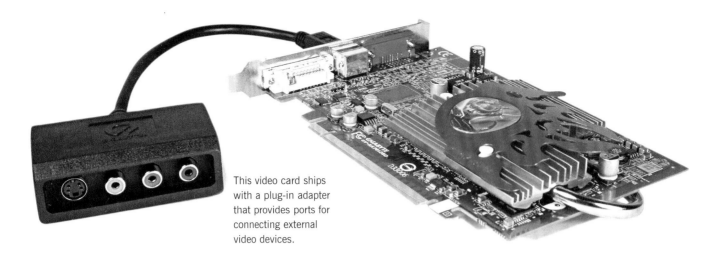

This video card ships with a plug-in adapter that provides ports for connecting external video devices.

Optional extras

As well as broadcasting pictures to a monitor, a video card can be put to other uses. These include:

- **TV-out** Hook up your computer to a TV set instead of a monitor to watch movies on the big screen.
- **Video in** Transfer video from an analogue video device such as a VCR or a camcorder onto the hard disk.
- **TV tuner** Connect an aerial and you can watch TV on your PC.
- **Dual-monitor support** Connect two monitors simultaneously for a widescreen effect.

For full details of what's possible with a video card and for tests and reviews of all the latest hardware, go to **www.tomshardware.co.uk/graphics.**

HDMI

If you've looked at a flat screen TV recently or upgraded from a DVD player to a Blu-Ray one, you've probably encountered an HDMI cable. HDMI – short for high-definition, multimedia interface – is designed specifically for connecting home entertainment equipment and it's an increasingly common sight on motherboards. The big advantage of HDMI is that sound and video are transferred via a single cable, although you do need to know about another acronym: HDCP.

HDCP

High-bandwidth, digital content protection (HDCP) is designed to prevent people from making unauthorised copies of digital content, such as movies or Blu-Ray DVD. The standard encrypts – scrambles – the signal as it moves from one device to another and only authorised devices can then unscramble it. Any TV with the 'HD Ready' logo should have HDCP built into it, so if you want to play media such as Blu-Ray discs on your PC and watch them on an HD TV then you'll need to ensure your graphics card supports HDCP. Most do, but you should always check.

SLI technology – what it is and why you should immediately forget about it

'Imagine tearing through today's most advanced PC games with an unheard of 48 gigapixels per second of raw graphics performance, 6 teraflops of compute [sic] power, 96 pixel pipes and an astounding 2GB of on-board graphics memory,' babbles graphics card manufacturer NVIDIA at **www.slizone.com/object/slizone_gf7950_gx2.html**. 'You don't have to imagine any more – this kind of power is available TODAY!' No, we've no idea what NVIDIA's on about either, but we do know it's got something to do with SLI.

Scalable Link Interface (SLI) is a way to run two extremely powerful NVIDIA graphics cards in the same PC (rival firm ATI has its own version of the technology, which it calls CrossFire). The benefits to the manufacturer are obvious – instead of selling you one stupidly expensive graphics card, SLI means it can sell you two – but what are the benefits to you? Er, none really. Unless your software's designed for SLI (or CrossFire), you can actually end up with poorer performance than with a single graphics card and, unless you're a keen PC gamer with a monitor the size of a house or you've been given the job of animating Shrek 4 from scratch, you almost certainly don't need SLI.

SLI (and rival standard CrossFire) enables you to connect two graphics cards together. It's almost certainly overkill for home computing.

Optical drives

The 'average' shop-bought PC these days has two optical drives: a CD-RW drive and a DVD-RW drive. In fact, the rapid uptake in recordable DVD after a shambolic start has been the only significant shift in optical technology recently, to the point where a DVD writer is *de rigueur* and no doubt about it.

Interface

If your motherboard has two IDE/ATA controllers, as is the norm, you can connect two devices to each. Typically you would install the HDD on the motherboard's primary channel (IDE1) and have your CD and DVD drives share the secondary channel (IDE2).

However, as we have discussed already, the IDE/ATA interface is gradually being phased out in favour of SATA. Although CD and DVD drives have no practical use for the increased bandwidth that SATA provides, it is possible – and indeed sensible – to buy a drive with a SATA socket rather than IDE/ATA. This ensures that you'll be able to reuse the drive in a future PC that uses a SATA-only motherboard. It also saves all that fuss with jumpers and helps keep the inside of your computer case tidy and cool.

To play music on audio CDs or a DVD movie soundtrack through the computer's speakers, you can connect the drive's analogue or digital audio output to one or other of the sound card's audio inputs (or directly to an analogue or digital socket on the motherboard if your motherboard has integrated audio). That said, in virtually every case you can forego this cable completely and allow the computer to extract audio directly and digitally through the IDE/ATA or SATA bus (see p.139).

Looking at a typical drive from a less flattering angle, from left to right we see the digital (small) and analogue (larger) audio cable sockets, the jumper pins, the IDE/ATA ribbon cable socket and finally the 4-pin Molex power socket.

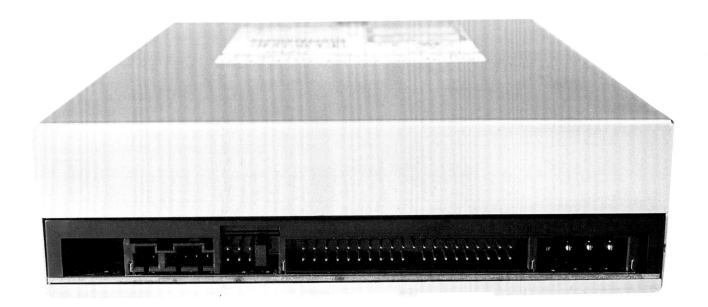

CD and DVD

A plain CD-ROM drive can read and play CDs but a CD-RW drive lets you make your own. There are two types of media: CD-R discs that, once full, can not be erased or re-recorded and CD-RW discs that can be reused time and time again.

To read DVD discs, be they data, audio or movie, you need a DVD-ROM drive. But if you want to make your own DVDs, you need a DVD writer – and that's where the fun begins …

Recordable DVD

There are three distinct DVD recording technologies around: DVD-R/-RW (the 'dash' or 'minus' formats), DVD+R/+RW (the 'plus' formats) and DVD-RAM. The R stands for recordable, in the sense that you can use a blank disc just once; while RW denotes Rewriteable, which means you can erase a disc and reuse it.

Each format has its pros, its cons, its proponents and its detractors.

- To backup and safeguard your own files, any format will do just fine. You needn't worry about compatibility issues if sharing your discs is not an issue.
- To turn a video file into a DVD movie that you can watch on the DVD player in your living room, check which recordable DVD technology the player can read and buy a drive to match. DVD-R/-RW has the widest drive/player compatibility, DVD+R/+RW runs a close second and DVD-RAM is incompatible with most DVD players. That said, in recognition of recordable DVD's popularity, more and more DVD players are offering support for all formats. This means that compatibility is no longer the burning issue it once was.
- Many DVD drives now also support all recording formats, which means you can throw just about any recordable media at them and emerge with a perfectly playable DVD. A multi-format drive is a smart choice.

Recording/writing/burning (one and the same) your own audio, data and video CDs is a breeze. Windows XP supports basic CD recording without the need for any third-party software.

- So too is a drive that supports dual-layer recording in the +R format. When paired with a dual-layer disc, this increases capacity from 4.7GB to 8.5GB. That equates to more movies or files per disc and, importantly, makes for easier backups. And with a double-sided dual-layer disc, you can go all the way to 17GB per disc.
- All DVD writers can record CDs, too. You may therefore feel that a single drive is all you need in new system. Indeed, if you're building a small form factor PC, one drive is all you'll have room for. The only real disadvantage is that you can't perform direct disc-to-disc copying when you have but the one drive. However, this limitation is not fatal: any decent recording software will extract an 'image' (copy) of the original disc, save it on the hard drive, then copy it onto a blank disc later.

A recordable DVD drive looks just like a CD drive but there's a power of technology packed into that case. This is a dual-layer multi-format model.

TECHIE CORNER

The technical differences between CD and DVD technology are many and microscopic, although you wouldn't think so from appearance alone. But the practical difference is really just one of storage space. A CD can hold between 650 and 700MB of data but DVDs start at 4.37/4.7GB and, in the double-sided, dual-layer format, reach all the way up to 15.9/17.1GB.

The either/or figures are due to a confusion over what a gigabyte actually is in the context of DVDs: either 1,073,741,824 bytes or 1,000,000,000 bytes, depending who you ask. The higher capacity figures (4.7 and 17.1GB) are based on the straight 'billion bytes' definition. On a computer, however, one gigabyte of data is always defined as 1,024 x 1,024 x 1,024 bytes (= 1,073,741,824 bytes). The net result is that a data gigabyte is bigger than a DVD gigabyte.

The consequence? You can only fit 4.37GB of computer files on a 4.7GB DVD.

Speed

Here's something not to worry about: read and write speeds. All recordable drives carry a cluster of speed ratings which refer to how quickly they burn discs of different formats. The very first generation of CD-ROM drives read data at a top rate of 150KB/sec and faster speeds are expressed as a multiple of this speed: 2x, 4x and so on. For instance, a 40x-speed drive can read data at 6,000KB/sec. Drives are usually slowest at writing data (or recording – it means the same thing) but there's not much in it these days.

DVD-ROM drives are also speed-rated. However, the base speed here is 1,385KB/sec, which is about nine times faster than an original CD drive. A 16x-speed DVD drive thus reads data at a rate of over 21MB/sec. Not that you really need this kind of speed in everyday use; a 1x DVD drive is adequate for movie playback. Again, recording speeds are slower but usually plenty fast enough.

By way of example, here are the speed ratings for the drive we use in our two PC projects later:

Media	Read speed	Write speed
CR-ROM	48x	-
CD-R	48x	48x
CD-RW	48x	24x
DVD-ROM	16x	-
DVD-R	16x	16x
DVD-RW	16x	6x
DVD+R	16x	16x
DVD+RW	16x	8x
DVD+R dual-layer	16x	4x

DVD is dead. Or is it?

In the previous edition of this manual, we said that 'two new kinds of disc hope to replace DVD in everything from PCs to video players: Blu-Ray and HD-DVD'. We weren't impressed, predicting that 'one format will thrive and the other one fail. Unfortunately, nobody really knows which one will be the winner, so... we'd suggest sitting this one out until a victor emerges.'

We were right: HD-DVD has gone to the great technology graveyard in the sky, leaving Blu-Ray as the only DVD replacement around. However, we're still not convinced that Blu-Ray is worth installing in your PC when DVD drives (and blank DVD discs) are so cheap. Unless you intend to back up lots and lots of data (Blu-Ray discs can store 25–50GB on a single disc) or connect your PC to a massive, high-definition TV in order to watch movies, there's no compelling reason to choose Blu-Ray over good old DVD.

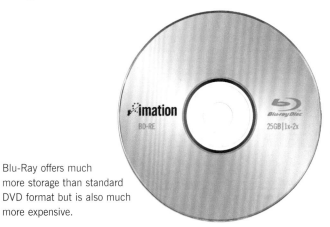

Blu-Ray offers much more storage than standard DVD format but is also much more expensive.

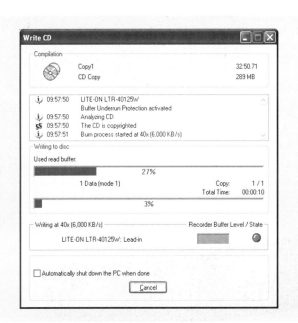

?

QUICK Q&A

What are the benefits of a high-speed drive?

Well, you can install software programs and burn your own CDs and DVDs more quickly in a fast drive. That's about it. The fact is that optical drive speeds have reached a practical plateau and are unlikely to get any faster until the next optical technology comes along.

Meanwhile, the faster a recordable drive runs, the greater the risk that the computer will fail to provide it with sufficient data to keep its laser burning continuously. The slightest pause or stutter used to mean a wasted disc and you'd have to start again. However, just about every drive now comes with some form of buffer under-run protection that alleviates the problem. You can minimise the risk further by leaving your PC to concentrate on the task at hand when it's busy burning a disc rather than attempting to multitask.

Buffer under-run protection (or burn-proofing) is built into most CD and DVD writers these days and dramatically reduces the number of spoilt discs they churn out.

Other possibilities

There's no shortage of potential add-ons and optional extras for a fledgling computer. Here we discuss a few essentials and suggest some other possibilities.

Modem

Before broadband internet access became widely available, a modem was a must-have – you couldn't get online without it. However, these days broadband is cheaper and much, much faster than old-fashioned dial-up internet access; as a result, the only time you need a traditional modem is if you live in a remote bit of the country where broadband isn't available.

If you get broadband, you might still get a modem – a cable modem for cable broadband or an ADSL modem for telephone line broadband – but they're not really modems as we know them; they're usually devices that plug into a spare USB port and connect to your broadband socket in the wall. In most cases you get them free when you sign up with a broadband Internet Service Provider.

A DSL or cable modem will generally be supplied as part of any broadband internet deal but you may need to install your own analogue modem for dial-up internet access.

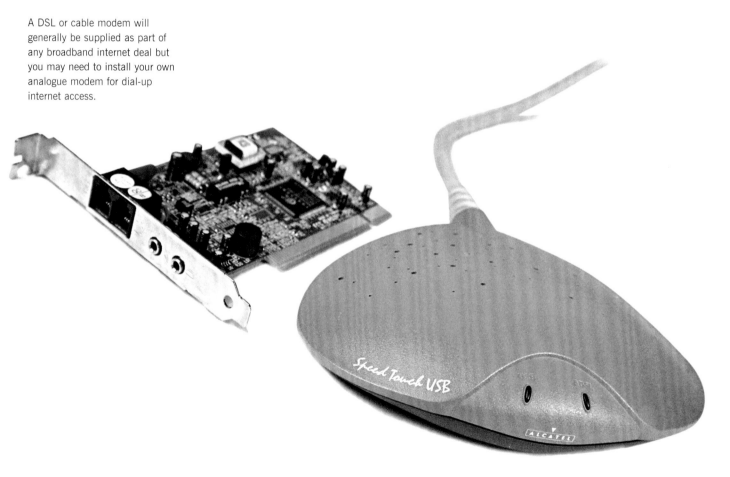

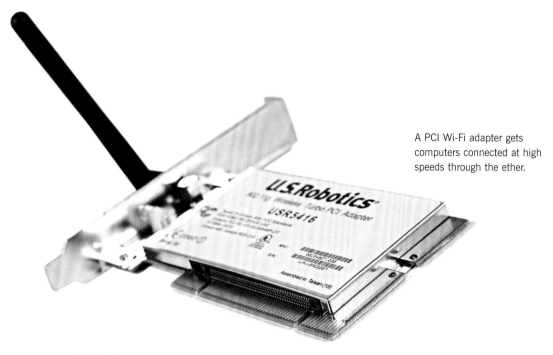

A PCI Wi-Fi adapter gets computers connected at high speeds through the ether.

Wireless networking (Wi-Fi)

If you want to connect PCs without running network cables everywhere, Wi-Fi - wireless networking - can cut the clutter. This is essentially Ethernet without wires, and there are four main standards: 802.11a, b, g and n.

802.11b is the most widely supported standard, but it's also the slowest, with a theoretical maximum speed of 11Mb/sec. 802.11g is faster at 54Mb/sec and also supports the slower 802.11b kit; and 802.11n is faster still, delivering speeds in excess of 100Mb/sec. It has better range, too, and it's less prone to interference. Last and definitely least there's 802.11a, which runs at 54Mb/sec but won't play nicely with the other 802.11 standards.

Many motherboards now include built-in Wi-Fi, usually 802.11b and 802.11g.

FireWire (IEEE-1394)

FireWire is a high-speed (50MB/sec) interface particularly suited to transferring digital video from camcorder to computer or for connecting fast external drives. Need we say that FireWire is increasingly supported by motherboards?

It's an Apple trademark but FireWire works just as well on a PC as a Mac. If your motherboard comes up short, install a PCI expansion card.

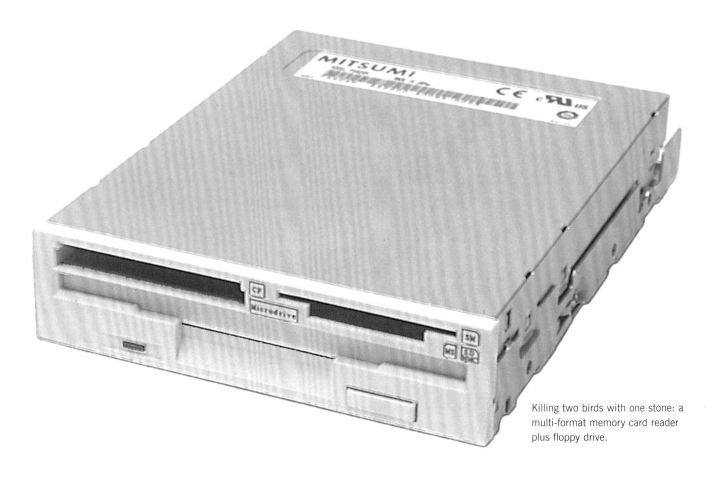

Killing two birds with one stone: a multi-format memory card reader plus floppy drive.

Games controllers come in all shapes and sizes, from a simple joystick to this (whatever it may be).

Media card reader

If you have a digital camera or a PDA (Personal Digital Assistant, or handheld computer), chances are it stores images and other files on a removable memory card. To transfer these files to your PC for editing, you can either connect the device with a cable – usually USB – or else plug the memory card into a card reader. You can get external card reading hardware, which is cumbersome, or internal models, which are convenient – particularly if it doubles-up as a floppy drive.

And the rest ...

A mouse, keyboard and monitor are definite givens, and a printer and scanner are obvious peripherals. But how else might you augment your PC?

Headphones and microphone Listen to music or games and record your own voice – or anything else – with a microphone. Windows has a sound recorder built-in but your sound card's software is likely to be more advanced. For use with speech recognition software, the best bet is a quality headset with an earpiece and microphone combined.

Joystick or games controller. These usually connect via a USB port but you can also get cordless models for greater flexibility.

This PCI expansion card provides SATA sockets for additional hard drives.

IDE or SATA controller card Add extra channels to your motherboard and connect another couple of hard disk drives. Essential for RAID, unless your motherboard provides native RAID support, and handy for massive storage requirements.

UPS (Uninterruptible Power Supply) Protect your files from power cuts with a UPS. Basically, it's a mini-generator that kicks in when the lights go out.

If the lights go out unexpectedly, will your data go with them? Not if you invest in a UPS.

Bluetooth A Bluetooth adapter lets your computer 'talk' to and exchange files wirelessly with other Bluetooth-enabled devices, notably mobile phones and PDAs.

PART 2 The perfect PC, mark 1

We're going to build two computers from scratch: a very powerful, full-size PC in a standard tower case and a tiny PC for home entertainment.

Making choices

The basic decision-making process looks like this:

- **Pick your processor** The latest quad-core processors pack a lot of power but they're expensive too: a dual-core processor provides more than enough horsepower for everyday computing, whether it's an Intel chip or an AMD one. The choice of Intel or AMD will dictate the kind of motherboard you need.
- **Choose your memory** DDR2 is the one you'll probably need (unless you're building a really high-performance system with the very latest processors, in which case you may need DDR3). The more memory the merrier: 1GB is the lowest you can really get away with, while 2GB is the sweet spot for Windows. You don't really need 4GB unless you're planning to do incredibly demanding tasks such as making a Hollywood blockbuster.
- **Integrated sound and graphics** Do you want a motherboard that includes a sound card and a video card or would you rather choose the sound and video systems separately? Integrated solutions slash the cost of building a PC but some of them will have an impact on performance.
- **Choose the form factor** ATX and a tower case is the Ford Focus of computing: it's widely available and very straightforward. We're going to use ATX for our bigger PC but we'll use a smaller form factor for our home entertainment machine.

Once you've settled these issues, the next step is to find a good motherboard with a chipset that provides all the right features. The main factors to consider, check, double-check and check again are:

- **Processor support** What socket does the motherboard have? What processor clock speeds does it support? What is the top FSB speed? If you're going for an older processor, will you be able to upgrade it later without replacing the motherboard too?
- **Memory support** What type of RAM does the motherboard need and how fast can it run? How much memory can you install? Are there any important restrictions?
- **Multimedia** Is there a 16x-speed PCI Express slot for a modern graphics card? If the motherboard has integrated graphics and you intend to stick with that for now, is there a spare PCI Express slot for future upgrades? If the motherboard has an integrated sound system, does it deliver surround sound or plain old stereo?
- **Hard disk support** Does the motherboard support IDE/ATA or Serial ATA? Both would be ideal.
- **Inputs and outputs** How many PCI expansion slots does the motherboard provide? Are there sufficient USB sockets? Do you need integrated networking or wireless networking?

- **Form factor** Will the motherboard fit in the case? ATX motherboards fit happily in ATX cases, but for smaller form factors you'll need a smaller motherboard too, such as a MicroATX model.

Our chipset choices

For our main PC, we've decided to build a high-end and very expandable PC based around a Core 2 Duo processor. It needs to be fast enough to edit video (and with storage capacity to match – video files are massive) but not so loud that it deafens us when we're running. We went for Core 2 Duo because our preferred motherboard has an Intel chipset that supports DDR2 RAM, Serial ATA and PCI Express, although an AMD Athlon 64 X2 would have worked just as well.

Our choice is a Gigabyte motherboard (the GA 965P DS3) based on the Intel P965 Express chipset, which can cope not just with the hardware we're adding today but which has plenty of room for expansion in the future. We are not recommending Gigabyte over other motherboard manufacturers, though – it just happened to be the best board in our price range for the things we wanted to do.

There's a very good chance that by the time you read this, the particular motherboard we chose will have been superseded, because motherboard firms like to update their model ranges very frequently. Don't get too hung up on the model numbers: what's important is the form factor and socket type. For example, the Gigabyte GA-P31-ES3G supports the same dual core processor and Serial ATA disk drives, includes a high-definition audio system and has lots of expansion room, but as it's more recent it runs a bit more quickly than the motherboard we've used.

Choosing the motherboard is the tricky bit; once you've got it, everything else is easy. Here's what we ended up with.

Component	Manufacturer	Model/specification	Notes
Motherboard	Gigabyte	GA 965P DS3	A standard ATX motherboard, so it should fit in our ATX case. It includes integrated audio delivering eight channels of surround sound and it supports both the latest processors and the latest memory technology.
Processor	Intel	Core 2 Duo E6700	This dual-core processor is right in the middle of the current Intel range, running at 2.67GHz, and it's very, very quick. If money's tight the motherboard also supports Pentium 4 CPUs.
Case	Akasa	AK-ZEN01-WH	A white midi-tower that's prettier than most, which has two internal fans and which promises to be quieter than the typical case. We actually wanted the black one, but it was out of stock everywhere we looked.
PSU	Akasa	AK-P050FG7-BKUK	This serious looking 500W power supply gives us lots of room to spare if we add hungry components in the future. Like the case, Akasa promises its PSU is quieter than most.
Memory	Crucial	BL2KIT12864AA80	These are two sticks of DDR2, 800MHz PC2-6400 RAM at 1GB apiece, the fastest kind of memory our chosen motherboard supports.
Hard disk	Samsung	HD400LJ	At 400GB the Samsung drive should have more than enough room for our home video files, even at high quality settings and, with a spin speed of 7,200RPM, it's quick too – which is essential for video.
Floppy disk	DabsValue	53-in-1 card reader	Floppies are dead but, thanks to digital cameras and mobile phones, memory cards are everywhere – so why not put a card reader in your floppy drive's place? That's what we're going to do.
DVD drive	LiteOn	SH-16A7S-053	A cheap, cheerful and very capable SATA DVD reader and burner that's compatible with all the major formats.
Sound card	n/a	n/a	Included on motherboard.
Video card	Sapphire	11095-03-2DR	An extremely powerful bit of kit, and just what you need when you're working with video. This card is a Radeon X1950 Pro with a very respectable 512MB of RAM and a PCI Express interface. It has its own cooling fan and needs a direct connection to our PC's power supply.
TV Tuner	Hauppauge	WinTV Nova-T 500	This PCI card enables our PC to receive TV broadcasts, including Freeview ones. It's got twin tuners, which means we can record one programme while watching another, and it also supports digital radio.

The perfect PC, mark 2

You don't need to build a huge beige box: PCs come in all shapes and sizes and you can choose from a dizzying array of cases. If you want a PC that won't look out of place in your living room, or that doesn't take up your entire house, then a small PC can be beautiful.

We've already designed an all-singing, all-dancing, multimedia marvel that's capable of dealing with absolutely anything. Now we're going to design a small PC that would sit happily in your living room or in a small spare corner. The days when small PCs couldn't do much are long gone and you can build a surprisingly powerful PC for very little money.

Of course, there are a few compromises. Smaller PCs don't have quite as much expansion room as full-sized ones and, while the process of building one is straightforward enough, some of the connections can be a little bit fiddly. However, as we'll discover in this section, you can cram an awful lot of technology into a very small space – without spending very much money.

Small PCs: what you need to think about

Before you start planning your small PC, it's important to think about what you want it to do. If it's going to be a general-purpose PC on a desk, then there are very few limitations on what you can build. If you want to put it under your TV, on the other hand, it's worth considering a few issues. Physical size is probably the most important one: if you want your PC to blend in with your other home entertainment kit, it's a very good idea to measure the available space and choose a case that will fit! Don't just look at the case dimensions, though: you'll need to add a few inches at the top, side and back of the PC to allow air to circulate. If you don't, your new PC could easily overheat.

If you're planning to use your small PC as a multimedia machine to take advantage of services such as the BBC iPlayer, Apple's iTunes or other online services, it's worth thinking about how you're going to connect your PC to the internet. In most houses the phone socket, which is where you connect your internet modem or router, is nowhere near the TV. That leaves you with a few options. We wouldn't recommend wireless networking – it's too slow for video, especially high-definition video – so you can do one of two things. You can run a very long Ethernet network cable from your PC to your broadband router or modem, which will involve running cables underneath the floor or drilling holes through walls, or you can invest in a Powerline network – also known as HomePlug, or HomePlug AV. This is an enormously clever technology that takes advantage of your house's mains wiring and enables you to connect your computers via normal plug sockets.

You need two adapters to create a Powerline network: one plugged into the wall next to your broadband router or modem, and one plugged into the wall next to your PC. Then it's just a matter of running an Ethernet cable the few inches between the PC and the adapter. Is Powerline networking a good idea? We

Cases come in all shapes and sizes. Make sure the one you choose has enough room for your chosen components!

think so. It's very easy to set up, you don't need to fill your house with unsightly cabling or drill through walls and, unlike a wireless network, it delivers more than enough speed for high-definition video. The downside is that the bits can be pricey: expect to pay between £60 and £100 for a pair of Powerline adapters and around £50 for additional adapters if you decide you want to connect other devices in the future.

The other thing to think about is what you're likely to use your PC for. If you plan to use your PC for home entertainment then it's a good idea to think about the connections you'll need, such as audio connections for home cinema speakers or an HDMI port so you can connect your PC to a flat-screen TV. If you want to use your PC as a digital video recorder, you'll need to invest in a TV tuner card too. We haven't done that with this PC, but we did with the bigger PC we designed in the previous section.

As with all PC building, don't just think about what you're going to do now: think about what you're going to do in the future too. Are you likely to connect your digital camera or camcorder to your PC? A case with USB ports on the front will make that much easier. Will you want to install additional hardware such as another hard disk or a TV tuner card? It might be a good idea to pick a case that has sufficient extra room for those components.

What we went for

We decided to build a small PC that could connect to our TV and store all our home videos, photos and music. That means we had some very specific requirements. We needed a motherboard with an HDMI display connection in addition to the usual

monitor connections so we could connect it to our TV; we needed a really big hard disk, because video files are massive; we needed enough graphics horsepower to run high-definition video on a big TV screen and a good quality sound card to make the soundtrack as good as the picture. Most importantly of all, we needed it to be cheap.

Because we wanted to build a small PC, we knew we couldn't get away with a standard ATX case and motherboard. Instead, we went for Micro ATX, which crams the same technology into less space.

The first thing to decide upon was the motherboard and processor combination. We shopped around for Micro ATX motherboards and discovered the Asus M3N78-VM, which includes a very powerful built-in graphics card and a high-definition sound card. Crucially, it also had an HDMI socket for our TV. The Asus motherboard is an excellent board and exceptionally good value for money: at the time of writing it was £50, which isn't much when you consider that you're also getting high-quality audio and graphics. While many motherboards' integrated graphics aren't particularly good, this motherboard includes an NVIDIA GeForce graphics processor – which is more than capable of running full-screen, high-definition video. That means we didn't need to buy an additional graphics card.

Next, we needed to choose a processor. This particular board is designed to work with AMD chips and it's compatible with a range of AMD processors designed to fit an AMD Socket AM2+ slot – so off we went to look at Socket AM2+ AMD processors. We decided on the AMD Athlon X2 7850, a dual-core processor running at a very impressive 2.8GHz. It was even cheaper than the motherboard: £44. The X2 isn't the most recent processor AMD makes, but the price of processors falls dramatically as newer ones are released. The 7850 delivers more than enough performance for the jobs we want our PC to do and, because our motherboard is compatible with a huge range of AMD chips, we can easily install something even faster in a few years.

Once we'd decided on our motherboard and processor, choosing the other bits was easy. The Asus board supports SATA disks, so we ordered a 1TB (1,000GB) Western Digital hard disk and a cheap and cheerful SATA DVD player–recorder. We checked the motherboard's memory support to discover that it used PC2-8500 memory chips, so we bought a pair of 1GB Ballistix memory chips from Crucial. 2GB is the sweet spot for running Windows Vista: 1GB isn't really enough to do anything demanding such as video, while anything more than 2GB isn't really necessary.

With the important bits of technology chosen, we needed to find a case to put it in. We went for the Antec NSK 1380, a cheap but robust and attractive case with a reasonable amount of room for expansion. It's a Micro ATX case, so we can be confident that our motherboard will fit and it has two drive bays: one for a DVD drive and one slightly smaller one – a 3.5-inch bay – for a hard disk. This is a standard size for hard disks, unless you're using a very unusual case.

The case has a built-in power supply unit, which saves a bit of money and a lot of time. While cases that come with a PSU are very handy, you need to be careful: if you're planning to install lots of expansion cards or a top-end graphics card, the power supply in a typical budget case won't be able to deliver enough power. At 300W, our case's power supply unit is perfect for the PC we're building; if you're going for advanced, power-hungry components, it's a good idea to buy your case and power supply unit separately. That's what we did with our bigger PC.

Our case isn't the smallest Micro ATX case you can buy. You can get fantastic-looking cases that are small, flat and wide, resembling DVD players, but we decided against them for two reasons. First of all, they can be expensive – our case was around £60, whereas home entertainment-style cases can be double that; more importantly, getting a PC into something so small means there are inevitably compromises. The main one is lack of expansion slots, because there simply isn't enough room for them. We want our PC to be as expandable as possible, so we'd rather have a slightly boxy-looking case than an ultra-slim one that we can't put expansion cards into.

Last but definitely not least, every PC needs an operating system. We built our PC just before Windows 7 was released, so we had to go with Windows Vista. That's not a problem: Windows 7 is really just a tweaked version of Vista, so the hardware we've chosen will work happily with Windows 7 – and the installation process will be identical. We chose the Home Premium edition, which includes excellent media features such as Windows Media Center, and we went for the 64-bit version.

Windows is available in 32-bit and 64-bit versions; if you have a 64-bit processor then 64-bit Windows takes full advantage of your hardware. We bought the OEM version, which comes without manuals and technical support but costs considerably less than the normal version you buy in PC World. It's worth pointing out that OEM copies of Windows are tied to a single computer: if you replace your PC in a few years, you need to buy a new copy of Windows.

Here's a quick reminder of the products we chose:

Component	Manufacturer	Model/specification	Notes
Motherboard	Asus	M3N78-VM	This is a Micro ATX motherboard, so it should fit happily in a Micro ATX case. It's also reasonably future-proof, with support not just for dual-core processors but also triple- and quad-core processors. It boasts high-quality, integrated graphics and sound and supports AMD Socket AM2+ processors. It also has stacks of connectors including plenty of USB ports and an HDMI port for a high-definition TV.
Processor	AMD	Athlon X2 7850 2.8GHz	A very fast dual-core processor. Requires a motherboard that supports AMD Socket AM2+.
Case	Antec	NSK 1380	A simple and attractive Micro ATX case with integrated power and enough room for expansion.
PSU	n/a	n/a	The case has its own 300W power supply, which is more than enough for our PC.
Memory	Crucial	Ballistix 1GB PC2-8500 DDR2 SDRAM	The motherboard supports up to four PC2-8500 memory chips. We've bought two at 1GB apiece. Our motherboard supports up to 8GB, although the 32-bit version of Windows can only handle 4GB.
Hard disk	Western Digital	1TB Caviar Black SATA WD1001FALS	Video files are massive but, with an incredible 1TB – 1,000GB – of storage, this drive won't run out of room any time soon. This is a SATA drive, which will work with our motherboard.
Floppy disk	n/a	n/a	Not required
DVD drive	LG	GH22NS40 Super Multi OEM	A cheap and cheerful DVD/CD player and burner, once again with SATA connections. We've chosen the OEM version, which doesn't include software or manuals but costs next to nothing.
Sound card	n/a	n/a	Included in motherboard
Video card	n/a	n/a	Included in motherboard

The nature of technology means that, by the time you read this, the various manufacturers will have updated their products – so Asus will have a slightly newer version of their motherboard with a slightly different model number, AMD will have newer, faster processors and so on. Don't worry about this too much: it's the combination of products that matters, not the specific model names. If you can't find the specific motherboard we've used in our PC, just look for Micro ATX motherboards with similar features and support for AMD Socket AM2+ processors; if you can't find the specific processor, see what other AMD Athlons (or faster Phenom chips – the motherboard supports them too) are available. As a rule of thumb, if you can't find the specific part we used here, you'll be able to get something even faster and more powerful for the same money.

3

PART **3**

Putting together a dual-core PC

Now, it's time to start building your computer – or in our case, computers. In this part, we'll build a dual-core desktop PC and, in Part 4, we'll create a tiny media PC for the living room. Although it's perfectly possible to build your entire computer in a few hours, you might prefer to start and stop at strategic intervals – so we've broken down the construction process into sensible sessions.

All set?

Just time for a couple of last-minute checklists.

Tooling up

There's no need to equip a workshop with expensive gadgets to build a computer. Here is a full and comprehensive list of all you will need.

- **Antistatic mat and wrist-strap** Electrostatic discharge (ESD) can do serious damage to motherboards and expansion cards, so protect your investment. At a minimum, we strongly recommend that you wear an antistatic wrist-strap whenever handling components. This should be clipped onto an unpainted bare metal part of the computer case. Better still, use an antistatic mat as well. In this case, you connect the wrist-strap cable to the mat and then connect the mat itself to the case. A component should be left safely ensconced within the antistatic bag it came in until you are ready to use it, and then rested on the antistatic mat before installation. Always – and we mean always! – unplug the power cable from the computer before commencing work.

Not a soldering iron in sight. You don't need a degree in electronics to fill a computer case with components.

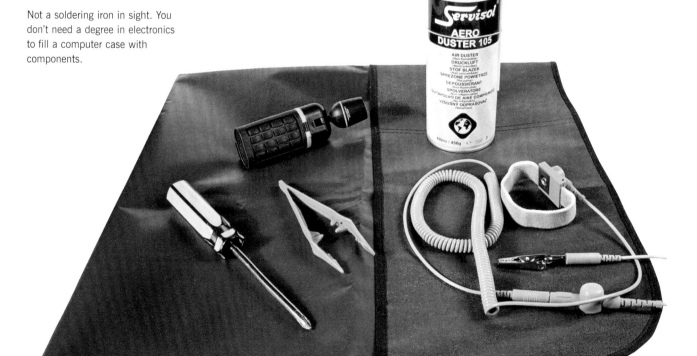

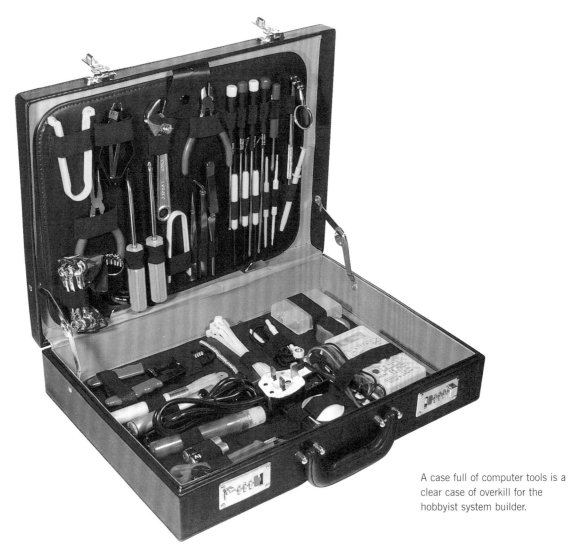

A case full of computer tools is a clear case of overkill for the hobbyist system builder.

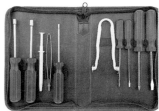

Ready-made screwdriver/pointy-thing kits like this one from Belkin are ideal.

- **Screwdrivers** A couple of Phillips and flat-head screwdrivers will suffice.
- **Pliers** Get hold of a pair of plastic pointy pliers or other pick-up implement for setting jumpers and retrieving dropped screws.
- **Air duster** A can of compressed air is more of an ongoing maintenance tool than a construction aid, to be honest, but is useful for de-fluffing and unclogging second-hand components.
- **Adequate lighting** An Anglepoise or similar light is really useful. Ample daylight is a bonus and a small clip-on torch essential.
- **Patience** Tricky to illustrate on the page but an essential component in any successful PC project. It's best to accept from the outset that not everything will run entirely smoothly. We can guarantee that you will drop the odd screw inside the case, for instance, and it's a fair bet that you will hesitate when required to insert a memory module or heatsink with rather more force than seems reasonable. There's also a chance that something relatively minor – a forgotten cable here, a wrongly set jumper there, a loose connection anywhere – will set you back awhile and force a bout of fraught troubleshooting. But throughout the entire procedure, stay relaxed and think logically. Short of a hardware failure in a specific component, which is itself easily diagnosed, rest assured that your efforts will be rewarded.

PART 6 Installing the processor and heatsink

Putting the processor in place and attaching the heatsink is very straightforward, but it can also be a bit fiddly – so we think it's easier to do this step before you screw the motherboard into your PC case.

For this step, we'd strongly recommend using an antistatic mat and an antistatic wrist-strap to get rid of any static charge that might be hanging around your body, as such charges can be fatal to PC components. The instructions that come with the antistatic kit will explain how you can make sure it's properly earthed, and it's important to follow those instructions again to re-earth everything if you take a break and return to your PC project later. You don't need to be wearing a nylon shell suit and dancing around in deep pile carpet to build up enough static to fry an expensive component, and most hardware firms' warranties are null and void if you don't take adequate protection and accidentally zap something expensive.

Some motherboards have a removable tray that you screw the motherboard to; if your case is one of them, then you should take that out of the case now and attach the motherboard to it before continuing. For standard PC cases, though, you can start with this section.

Unpack the motherboard and hold it gently by the edges, taking care not to touch any of its components: some of them are fairly fragile and it's all too easy for careless fingers to knock something important out of action. Place the motherboard on a flat, clean surface (or on your antistatic mat, if you have one). Occasionally you'll find that the motherboard manufacturer has stuck a sticker across some of the slots, which is the case here. Very gently, prise the sticker off the expansion slots and curse the genius who thought putting stickers on sensitive components was a smart thing to do.

2

Try to avoid leaving any residue from the sticker on the expansion slots, because it's a pain to get rid of. If there is some residue left when you've removed the sticker, gently scrape it off and make sure none of it falls inside the expansion slots themselves.

3

Locate the processor socket – if you have the motherboard facing towards you with its various input and output ports furthest away from you, the socket will be towards the right side of the motherboard. This is an Intel motherboard and the processor goes into a Socket 775 slot. The socket is protected with a metal cover and locked with a lever, so the first step is to unclip the lever and lift it up.

4

The socket cover is hinged at the back and should lift up easily. Be very gentle with the cover, as its hinges are easily damaged. Leave the cover up for now.

5

Once you've unlocked the processor, you should be able to remove the plastic protector. It's worth keeping hold of this: you'll need to put it back in if your motherboard turns out to be faulty and has to be returned to the manufacturer.

6

Holding your processor by the outside edges, look for the little gold triangle in one corner. There should be an accompanying indicator in the processor socket. Carefully line up the processor and gently lower it into place. Be extremely careful as you do this.

7

The processor should simply drop into position, and you'll know instantly whether it's been lined up correctly: if it has, a gentle press will make it sit securely in its socket and if it hasn't, it won't. You don't need to apply anything more than the lightest pressure to sit the processor in its socket and doing so would be a bad idea anyway: it'd bend the processor's pins, causing irreversible damage to it, to your motherboard or to both.

8

When you're confident that the processor is sitting happily in its socket, close the metal cover on top of it and use the lever to lock everything in place. The lever needs a bit of a push in order to close it. Remember to lock the lever in position by pushing it underneath the clip at the side of the processor socket.

9

And here's the result: one shiny new processor locked into its socket. You could connect the power at this point, but if you did the processor would immediately overheat and fry itself. Modern processors run at very high temperatures, so we'll need to fit a heatsink to keep it cool before we can do anything else. Provided you bought a retail processor and not a cheap, unpackaged OEM unit, the heatsink will be in the same box your processor came in. If you've bought an OEM chip, you'll need a separate heatsink and thermal paste to glue it to your processor.

This is our heatsink, and it's even heavier than it looks. The three stripes you can see on the bottom are the thermal paste that glues the heatsink to the top of your processor, and it's very important that you don't touch them or allow anything to touch them. When you handle the heatsink, hold it by its outside edges.

The heatsink has four 'legs', which are pins that fit into holes in your motherboard. Lift the heatsink over the processor socket and you should be able to see the appropriate holes. Gently lower the heatsink so each leg is in one of the holes.

Now for the scary bit. The manual says that you can now click the pins into place, but by click it means 'a horrendous cracking sound that makes you think you've snapped the motherboard'. The amount of pressure you need to use on each pin is truly frightening, but provided the motherboard is supported properly and can't bend, you'll be OK.

You'll know the pins have been inserted properly when you've heard four heart-stopping cracks as you push them into place and the heatsink doesn't move if you poke its legs. Under no circumstances attempt to move, let alone boot, your PC if the heatsink is not locked firmly into position. Doing so is a recipe for disaster.

13

You'll have noticed that the heatsink also includes a rather large fan, and you should never, ever, ever power up your PC if that isn't connected – doing so is a one-way ticket to meltdown city. The fan has a connector block attached to it, and this goes into the CPU_FAN socket on the motherboard – it's usually an inch or two away from the heatsink itself, on the very edge of the motherboard.

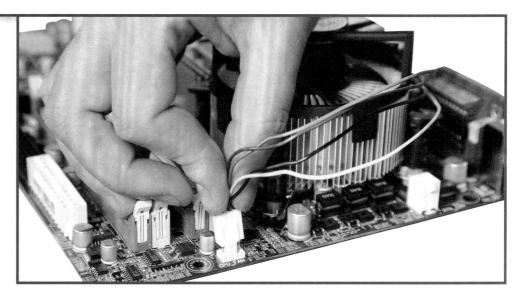

14

The heatsink's power cable is usually wrapped around the heatsink itself, and you might need to unwrap it a little bit so it reaches the motherboard connector. Just make sure that you don't unwrap it so much that the cable's likely to be hit by the fan blades as they spin or become snagged in other parts of the motherboard. Similarly, don't keep it so tightly wrapped that it bends the power connector on the motherboard. If that cable dies, your PC fries. Not a cheery thought.

PART 6

Installing RAM

Before we put the motherboard into our PC's case, we can install the memory modules: as with the processor, it's a little bit fiddly and it's much easier to do when the motherboard is sitting on a desk.

If your motherboard supports dual channel memory and you want to take advantage of it (which you should, because it delivers a significant performance boost), it's essential that your two or four RAM modules are identical. That means they need to run at the same speed and same capacity, and ideally they should come from the same manufacturer.

Once your heart's recovered from locking the heatsink into place, it's time to insert your memory chips. Depending on the kind of motherboard and kind of memory you've chosen, the number and size of the memory banks may differ from what you see here, but the principle is just the same.

As you can see, our RAM sockets are colour coded: two of them are red and two of them are yellow. That colour coding helps you see where to put your chips, because if you're putting in a pair of RAM modules they need to go in specific slots to enable dual-channel performance. In the case of our motherboard, that means if you put the first RAM module in a yellow socket then you need to put the second one in a yellow socket too. Consult your motherboard manual to see which sockets you need to use for your memory – putting the modules in the wrong sockets does make a difference, so it's better to get it right first time. In the case of our motherboard, the manual says we should use the top, yellow socket first and then the second yellow socket for our second memory module.

To insert a RAM module, open the clips on either edge of the socket and then line up the module with the slot. Memory is shaped and will only fit one way, so gently push the module into the socket and make sure its pins line up properly. If they don't, lift it out, turn it back to front and try again.

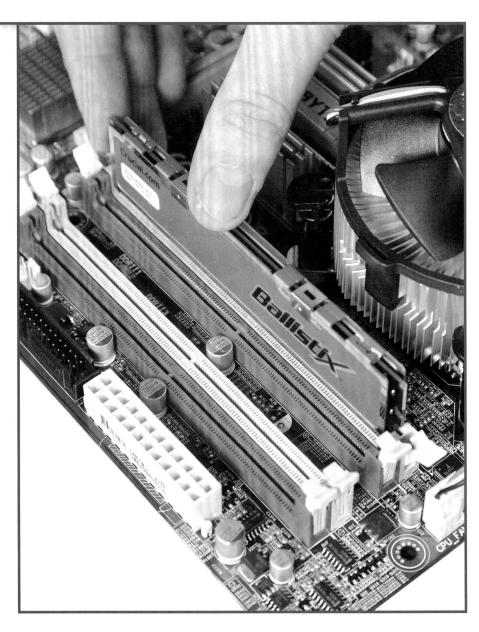

2

Time for another scary bit: to secure the RAM modules in place you'll need to apply a reasonable bit of force, because the sockets are a tight fit (deliberately so – you don't want the memory to fall out again if you move your PC).

Before you start shoving, make sure the module isn't round the wrong way – if it is, applying force could break the modules or your motherboard – and then apply pressure to each side of the module simultaneously. The module should now slide into place and the clips on the edges of the socket should lock automatically. If they don't, lock them manually with a quick flick of the finger.

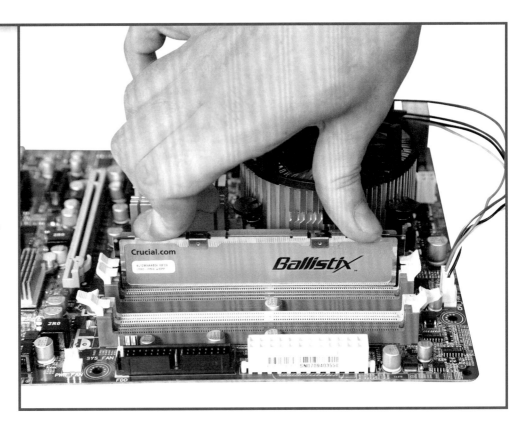

3

If you have a second memory module, the installation process is identical: line up the module, give it a good shove and lock it in place.

PART

Installing the motherboard

That's the scary stuff over with, so now we can put our motherboard into our PC. Things can get a little bit cluttered when you start adding disk drives, video cards and so on but, as we'll discover, it's all nice and simple.

If your computer case has a removable motherboard tray, you should attach the motherboard to it before doing anything else – and you'll be able to skip Step 4, where we screw little brass standoffs into the PC case.

QUICK Q&A

My motherboard doesn't fit!
Provided you've bought the right kind of motherboard – an ATX board to fit in an ATX case – then, while you might have difficulty lining up the various screws, it's unlikely that you've bought the wrong motherboard. It's much more likely that minor manufacturing errors mean that some holes are very, very slightly out of alignment. It's worth persevering: we've installed stacks of motherboards and we've yet to be beaten by one!

First things first: it's time to get the sides off the PC case so we can start sticking things into it. Different cases have different approaches; for example, some of them have fixing screws on the back that you'll need to unscrew with a star screwdriver, others have thumbscrews that you can loosen and remove by hand, and really fancy cases have a magic lever that you pull to unlock the case sides. The method doesn't matter: what does matter is that you get the sides off. We've only taken one side off, but you'll need to remove both in order to secure your hard disks and other peripherals.

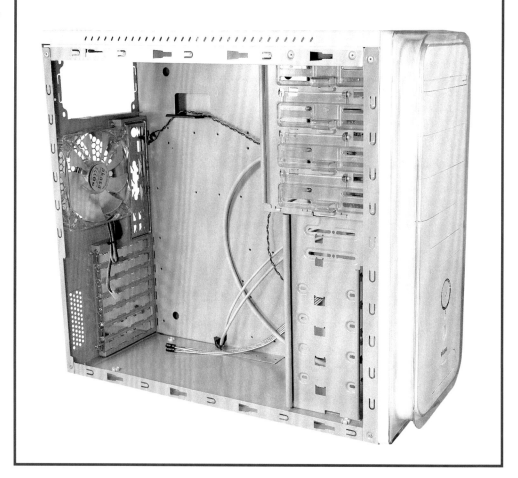

2

Turn the case around so you're looking at the back and you should see a blanking plate with spaces for connectors such as the keyboard, the mouse, the USB ports and so on. It's nice that it's there, but unfortunately the chances are that it's completely useless because it won't even vaguely match the connectors on the back of your motherboard. That means it needs to come out – and even more unfortunately, the only way to do that is to grab it with your fingers and give it a good yank. As the blanking plate is made of very thin metal, be very careful here or you'll end up giving yourself a cut.

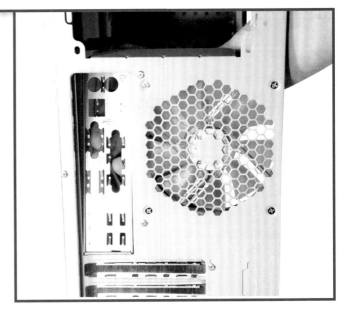

3

The packaging of your motherboard should include a spanking new blanking plate for the back of your PC case, and it's just a matter of putting it into place and pushing it until it snaps in. Again, watch your fingers. Make sure it's the right way up – in this photo, the top of the case is to the right – and be careful when you put it in place as the thin metal is all too easy to bend.

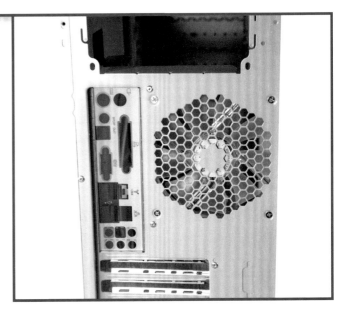

4

We're nearly ready to install the motherboard, but first we need to lay the case on its side so we can get easy access to its innards. When you've done that you'll see that there's a metal sheet inside the case for your motherboard to sit on, and it's got lots of little holes in it. The holes are for standoffs, little brass stands that screw into the tray and which you then screw the motherboard to, and you'll find dozens of them in a little bag that came with your case.

You don't need to put a standoff in every available hole, but you do need to put one in each hole that corresponds to a hole in your motherboard. The smart thing to do, then, is to hold the motherboard over the tray, identify which holes you need, and then screw in the appropriate standoffs. Don't be tempted to skip this step, no matter how dull it seems: it's essential that your motherboard is properly affixed to the case.

5

Once you've attached your bits of brass, it's time to put the motherboard in position. The easiest way to do this is to start from the back of your case by lining up its various ports and connectors with the blanking plate you just fitted. Once you've done this, gently lower the motherboard onto the brass standoffs.

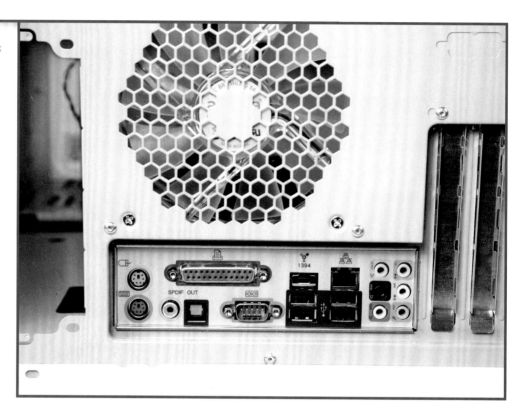

6

As you'd expect, once the motherboard's in the right position you need to screw it into place. Again, the screws you need will be in a little bag that came with your case. Don't be entirely surprised if you drop a screw doing this, because it's very fiddly – but don't use a magnetic screwdriver to fish it out or leave the screw inside your PC case forever.

7

Depending on the kind of case you've bought it will have one, two or even three fans to keep everything nice and cool. Although the connectors aren't marked they're easy enough to identify by simply finding the cables that snake from the fans. To connect a fan, plug its connector block into an appropriate space on the motherboard. There are several, marked SYS_FAN, PWR_FAN and so on.

8

If you have more than one case fan, you'll need to connect that too. The procedure is identical, but make sure you don't use the connection marked CPU_FAN – you should already have the heatsink plugged into that one!

9

In addition to its fans, your case has a bunch of connectors for the power button, the drive activity LED and so on. Although these connectors are marked, there's no clue as to which way round they should go – and it's the same on the motherboard, which tells you where to connect them but doesn't say which way round they need to go. Here, we've connected our various front panel cables and we're hoping they're all round the right way. In some cases it doesn't matter, but if any of the front panel features such as the reset button or LED doesn't work then it means you've got the connector back to front and you'll need to swap it round. It's easily one of the most annoying things about PC building.

10

More case connectors? We're afraid so. This time we need to connect the front audio panel, which provides handy access to the headphone and microphone socket. This one's nice and easy: on the motherboard you'll see a connector marked F_AUDIO, and that's the one you need to use.

Most cases also have front-mounted USB ports which, once again, are very handy. And once again, they need to be connected to the motherboard. As with the audio connector, the appropriate motherboard sockets are easy enough to find, and they're helpfully marked with the legend USB.

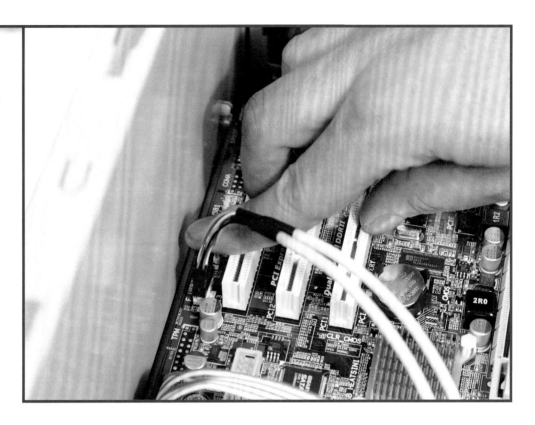

If you've got more than one front USB port you'll have more than one cable to connect. The second USB connector on your motherboard should be right next to the first one.

That's the various case components connected. Now, it's time for some power.

Installing the power supply unit

If your case came with a power supply unit preinstalled, then great. In most cases, though, you need to provide your own power supply unit. With smaller cases, if the PSU is already installed, you may need to remove it temporarily before you can fit the motherboard.

Once everything's connected, it's a good idea to connect the power cable to the power supply, plug the cable into the wall, press the switch on the back of the power supply unit to the On position and switch on the PC to make sure it's working (although of course you need to steer well clear from the insides – you don't want to electrocute yourself). If everything's connected properly, you should see the various fans spinning, including the one on the heatsink.

If your motherboard doesn't have integrated graphics (because you've done the same as we did and invested in a stand-alone video card) and you leave the PC running, you'll almost certainly hear a number of beeps after a few seconds. The beeps are giving you a fault code, which you can use to diagnose hardware problems.

If you're wondering why your PC beeps instead of just telling you what the problem is with an on-screen error message, it's because beeps are like the cockroaches of the computing world: they can survive almost anything. Provided your motherboard has power and you remembered to connect your PC speaker, your PC can make beeping noises even when other major components – the processor, the memory or the video card – aren't functioning. An on-screen message telling you your video card's not working is useless, because if your video card's broken or hasn't been connected correctly then you won't be able to see it.

Back to business. As we already know what the hardware problem is – we haven't put a video card into our PC just yet, so our PC is saying, 'Beep! No video card! Beep!' – there's no need to worry, but if you want to make doubly sure then refer to p.160 for our explanation of beep codes and what they're trying to tell you.

Before continuing, make sure you disconnect the power cable and switch everything off again. Never work on a PC that's plugged into the mains, even if the PC itself is switched off. Until you unplug the power cable, there's still enough electricity inside your PC to seriously ruin your day – so always double-check that you've disconnected the power before going anywhere near your PC's insides. Remember to re-earth your antistatic protection too. You can't be too careful.

Installing a power supply is nice and simple, although actually screwing it into place is a little tricky – and isn't helped by the fact that power supply units are much heavier than they appear. If your case has a shelf for the power supply to sit on – most do – you'll need to press it against that while simultaneously lining up the power supply unit's screw holes with the pre-drilled holes in your PC case. Once you've done that, you can screw the power supply into place. Make sure it's nice and tight because, if it isn't, your PC will quickly develop a really annoying rattle, but don't overtighten the screws or you may strip their threads, in which case they may work loose over time.

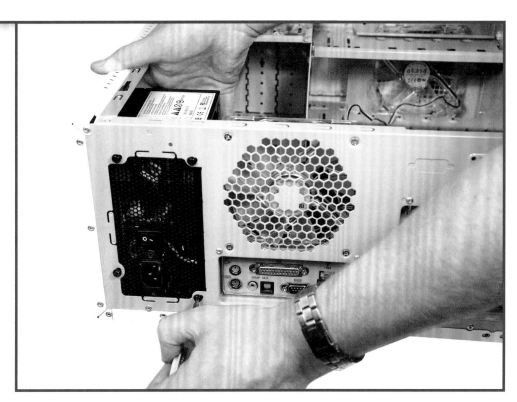

Once the power supply unit is in place, connect the motherboard power block to the appropriate socket on the motherboard. You can't miss it – it's a huge socket along the edge of the motherboard nearest the power supply unit, and the connector block is shaped so you can't put it in the wrong way round. Our motherboard takes the standard 24-pin connector that our power supply unit's mess of cables includes, but your PSU should also include an adapter that enables you to connect older motherboards that have a slightly different 20-pin connector design. If you're using an older motherboard with an early Pentium 4 processor, look for the ATX 12V connection too *(see p.49 for a picture).*

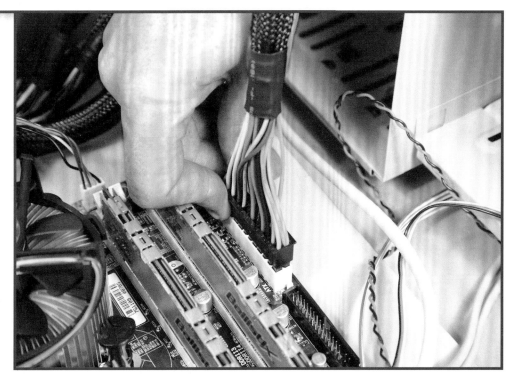

PART 5

Installing the DVD drive, card reader and hard disk

Installing DVD drives and hard disks is very straightforward, especially if they use the modern Serial ATA (SATA) connectors. Because SATA devices use a special power plug, though, it's essential that your power supply unit has the necessary power connectors for your SATA drives.

If you're using older IDE/ATA drives you'll make connections with big ribbon cables instead of the slim SATA cables in our PC, but the principle is the same. However, there's one crucial difference with IDE/ATA drives: jumpers. If two drives are going to share the same IDE/ATA channel, you need to set one as the master and one as the slave. To do this, you need to fit a plug called a jumper to connect two little pins on the back of the drive. The drive manual should tell you which pins to connect for the master and which for the slave, and the packaging should also include the jumpers themselves. If you can't see the jumpers, check the back of the drives: they're often fitted before the drive leaves the factory.

1

Many cases now include plastic securing brackets for your 5.25 inch drives, which means you don't have to muck about with screws when you want to secure your drive in an empty bay. Our case is one of those models, but before we can put our DVD drive into a spare drive bay we need to open the securing brackets on both sides of the PC case. Unclipping the brackets is simple: it's just a matter of giving the tab a gentle squeeze and then lifting up the bracket.

Once you've unclipped the securing brackets, turn your attention to the front of the case and pop off the plastic cover that sits over the drive bay you want to use. The cover is usually secured by two plastic clips, and if you reach inside the case and give both clips a squeeze you can then pop the cover off by pushing it outwards. Once you've done that it's just a matter of sliding the DVD drive into the hole by pushing it gently into place. You might need to use your other hand to hold the securing clips out of the way as you do this.

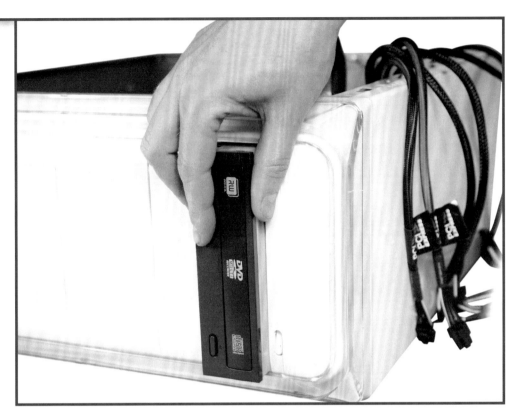

You'll see that on each side of the DVD drive there are screw holes. Line them up with the holes in the case itself and you should now be able to lock the securing clips in place by pushing them down until they lock. Don't push too hard – if the holes aren't lined up exactly with the pins in the securing bracket, trying to force the bracket to close will just break the pin. Gently move the drive around until the holes line up perfectly and the pin pops into place without any fuss – and remember to do the same with the bracket on the other side of the case.

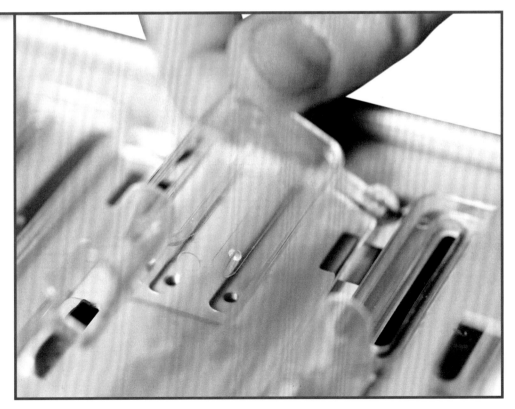

④

Installing the hard disk drive is essentially the same process as installing the DVD drive, but there are a few key differences. First, the hard disk is a 3.5 inch model, so we need to use one of the smaller drive bays further down the front of the case; secondly, there aren't any securing clips to worry about; and thirdly, you don't need to remove the front cover panel because you never need to see the front of your hard disk drive. Simply slide the hard disk drive into position and make sure its screw holes line up with the ones in the case's drive bay.

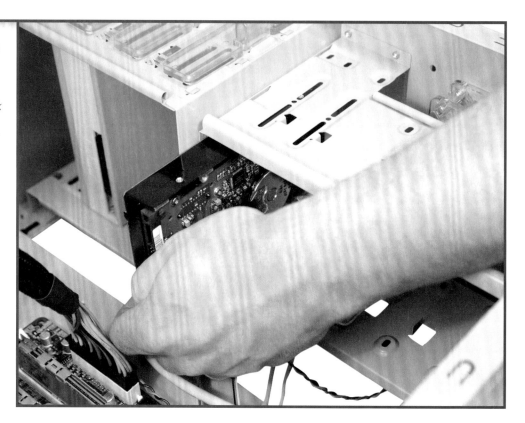

⑤

Because there aren't any securing brackets, we need to secure the hard disk drive using good old-fashioned screws, which should have come in a bag inside the hard disk packaging. Remember to put screws in both sides of the drive bay to avoid vibration and rattling.

6

Instead of a floppy disk drive, we'll install a multi-card reader, which sits in a spare drive bay. As with our DVD drive we need to unclip the securing clips, pop off the panel covering the drive bay and slide the card reader into place, but there's one important difference: it's a USB device, which means it needs to be plugged into a spare USB port – and those ports are outside the case. The answer's simple, though: there's a spare hole in the back of the case (it's designed for really old motherboards that have a serial port, which is a rarity these days), so we can pop its cover off and run the card reader's USB cable through that and connect it to one of the USB ports on the back of the PC.

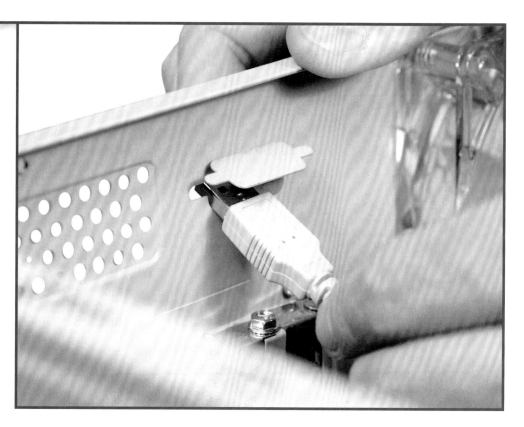

7

Now we need to give our drives some power. Our power supply unit has a mass of cables coming from it with a range of different connectors. One of those cables is an SATA power cable with connectors for two SATA devices. By a happy coincidence, our DVD drive and our hard disk are both SATA devices, so we can use the same power cable for both. You'll see that the cable has two power connectors, one in the middle and one at the very end; plug the middle one into the power socket in the back of the DVD drive.

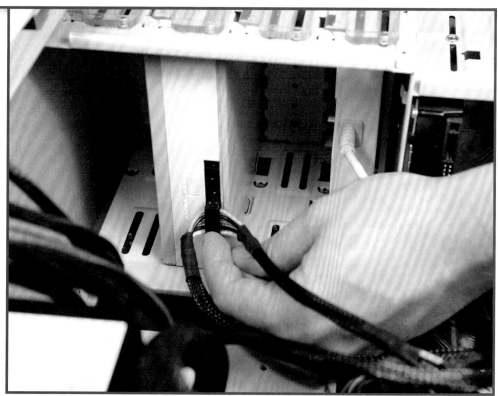

8

As you'd expect, the next step is to plug the connector at the end of the SATA power cable into the socket on the back of the hard disk drive. You've successfully added power to both of your drives. Now, it's time to add their data connections too.

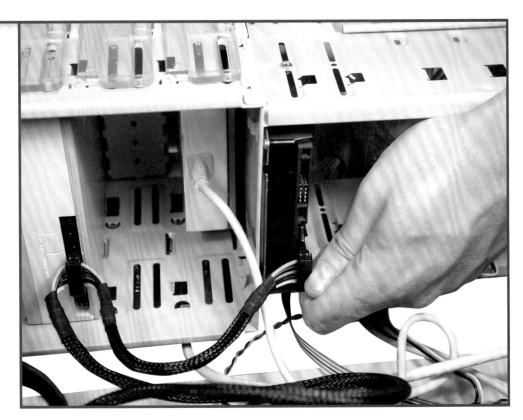

9

Your motherboard's packaging should include various extra cables and if, like ours, it supports SATA devices, those cables should include SATA data cables – which is handy, because we need them now. Take one of the cables and plug it into the SATA data socket in the back of the DVD drive. The cable is shaped so it can only be connected in one way. Now, take the second SATA data cable and connect it to the socket on the back of your hard disk.

Now, you need to plug the other ends of your SATA cables into the appropriate places on the motherboard. Take your first cable and look for the sockets marked SATA on the motherboard – on ours, they're near the front left corner of the motherboard and marked in bright colours. Once again the cables are shaped, so you can't connect them the wrong way round.

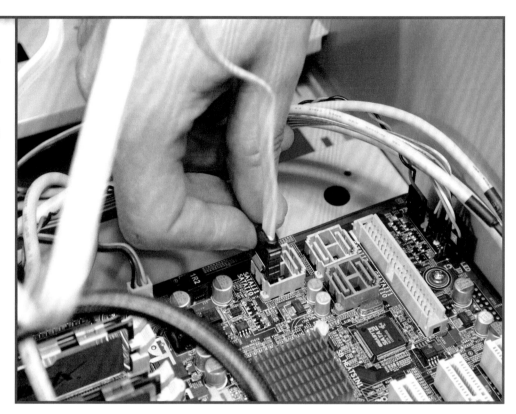

Repeat the process with the second SATA data cable. Your motherboard should now look like this, with twin SATA cables – one for the DVD drive, one for the hard disk – connected to the motherboard's SATA data connectors. It's worth checking the motherboard manual at this point because some older boards offer both high speed and slightly lower speed SATA connections, and you need to use the high-speed ones with the latest, fastest hard disks.

We're making excellent progress: we have a processor, we have RAM, we have power and we have storage. As the motherboard has its own integrated sound card, all that's left to do is add the video hardware. As we'll discover, that couldn't be simpler.

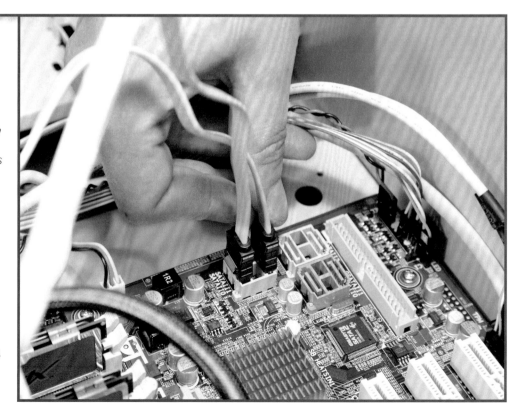

PART  # Installing the video card

Our PC is coming along nicely. We have a processor, we have power, we have memory and we have storage, so now it's time to add the video card. We'll also install a TV tuner card so we can use our PC as a digital video recorder.

The video card we've chosen is a PCI Express device and while it plugs into a spare slot like any other expansion card, it has a few unique things you need to watch out for. First of all, the tail – the end of the card furthest away from the back of the PC – needs to be locked in place, because such video cards are very heavy and would be unstable if they weren't locked into place. The same applies to AGP cards, the predecessor of PCI Express.

PCI Express cards also need a direct connection from the power supply, because the motherboard can't provide enough power for today's extremely demanding video technology.

Before you can install your video card, you need to make room for it. Every PC case has a selection of PCI slots, which are spaces for add-in cards such as video cards, but by default the places they go are covered up with metal plates to stop dust getting into the system. Before we can install our graphics card, then, we need to remove the plate that corresponds to the slot we're going to put our card in – in this case, the PCI Express slot, which is second from the right. To remove the plate, simply remove the single screw holding it in place (with some PC cases there's a clip instead of screws; just lift up the clip) and then remove the metal plate.

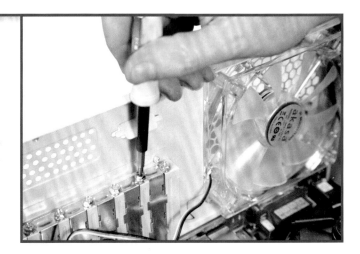

Remember how you had to apply a fair bit of force to insert your memory modules? It's the same with graphics cards. Check that the card's pins are lined up with the slot and then press down firmly to lock it into place. Once the card is in its correct position use the screw or clip that held the blanking plate in place to secure the video card.

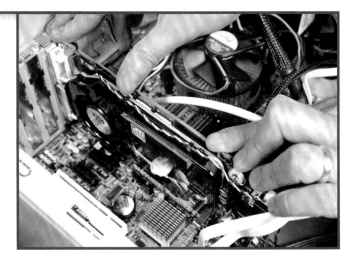

3

If, like us, you've gone for a PCI Express graphics card, it needs its own power supply and won't work without one. On this Sapphire card, like most PCI Express cards, the power socket is at the end nearest you (if you're looking at it from the front of the PC). Locate the appropriate cable running from the power supply unit and connect it to the graphics card's power socket.

4

In addition to our graphics card we'll also install a TV tuner card that enables our PC to receive TV broadcasts and act as a digital video recorder. As it's a standard PCI card, we don't need to connect a dedicated power supply but, as with our graphics card, we need to remove a blanking plate from the back of the PC, push the card into a spare slot and then use the screw or clip to anchor it in place.

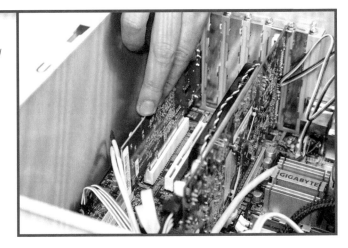

Congratulations – you've built an entire PC. All that's left to do now is a bit of tidying up. If your power supply unit came with cable ties (most do) it's a good idea to use them to keep spare cables out of the way and to ensure that no cables get too close to whirring fans or hot bits such as the processor's heatsink (see p.140 for more details of this). Once you've done that, you can replace the sides of your PC case, connect the keyboard, mouse and monitor and enter the very last stage of PC building: installing the operating system.

TECHIE CORNER

If your motherboard has onboard video and you plan to use it, you'll need to fit the VGA port bracket that came with your motherboard. The bracket includes a cable that plugs into the motherboard – the motherboard manual will tell you where to connect it – and it goes in place of one of the PCI blanking plates at the back of your PC.

If you decide to upgrade your graphics later on, you might need to disable the onboard graphics processor in your system BIOS. We say 'might' because many motherboards automatically disable onboard graphics when they detect a new graphics card. Your motherboard manual will tell you whether your particular board has this auto-detection feature or whether you'll need to fiddle with the BIOS.

We're ready to roll: our PC is ready to run and it's time to install the operating system so we can start using it.

PART

Building a small form factor PC

In the previous project, we could just as easily have used an AMD processor and virtually everything would have been identical save for a slightly altered processor and heatsink installation. But now it's time to build an altogether different PC. This time we will base it around an AMD Athlon X2 processor.

PART

Installing the processor and heatsink

As with our previous PC, the first step is to install the processor, heatsink and cooling fan. While we're using an AMD processor instead of an Intel one, installation is almost identical.

Before you start, make sure that all your components are the right ones – it's not unheard of for firms to deliver the wrong bits – and that you have all the components that you need. Pay particular attention to the motherboard and the case. The former should include not just the motherboard, but a CD or DVD with the necessary drivers for the video card, sound card and network card as well as two SATA data cables; the latter should include a packet of mounting screws of various shapes and sizes. Without the cables and screws you won't be able to finish building your PC, so make sure everything's there before you start!

Remove the motherboard from its packaging and put the additional cables somewhere safe. Once again we'd recommend using an anti-static wrist strap and mat to prevent any accidental damage to the motherboard.

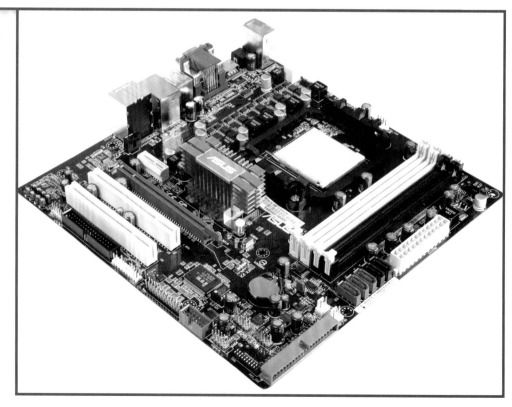

2

The CPU socket is easy to find: it's a big grey square roughly in the centre of the motherboard. The socket is secured by a lever, which is locked by default. Before we can insert the processor, we need to unlock the socket. To do this, simply lift it up and pull it. Make sure the lever is 90–100 degrees from horizontal or there won't be enough room for the processor's pins.

3

If you look very carefully you'll see an embossed triangle in one corner of the processor socket. This matches a triangle on the processor itself, and it's very important that when you insert the chip you put its triangle over this one.

4

Holding the chip by its edges – never handle a processor by touching its pins – gently place the processor in the socket. It should slot easily into place. If it doesn't, make sure the two triangles are aligned and that the lever is 90–100 degrees from the horizontal. You should never need to apply force to a processor: if you do, something's wrong and the force will damage the processor beyond repair.

When you're confident that the processor is in the right place, push the lever back down and ensure that it's in the locked position.

Now, we need to place the heatsink and fan on top of the processor. You'll notice some grey goo on the bottom of the heatsink: this is thermal paste, which ensures heat transfer from the processor to the cooling system.

Gently lower the heatsink assembly on top of the processor, ensuring that the metal clips on the heatsink fit on the plastic nubs of the motherboard. If the clips aren't in the right place, you won't be able to lock the heatsink in position.

Pull the lever on the clip down to lock the heatsink and fan into place. This takes a surprising amount of pressure but, provided the clips are in the right place, you don't need to worry about damaging anything.

If you've lined everything up correctly, the heatsink clips should look like this. It's very important that everything is in the right position here: if it isn't, your processor won't be cooled properly and you'll encounter problems in the future.

You'll notice a cable connected to the processor fan. This is the power cable; if it isn't connected, your PC will overheat within seconds of switching your PC on. Locate the CPU_FAN connector on the motherboard and connect this cable to it.

PART

Installing the memory

This bit couldn't be easier: Asus has helpfully colour coded its motherboard, so you can see exactly where your chips need to go, and the chips and memory slots are shaped so you can't put the memory modules in the wrong way.

On our motherboard there are four memory slots. If you have one or two memory chips to install, you should insert them in the yellow slots first. Each slot has a pair of clips, one at either end. Use your finger to flick them open before continuing.

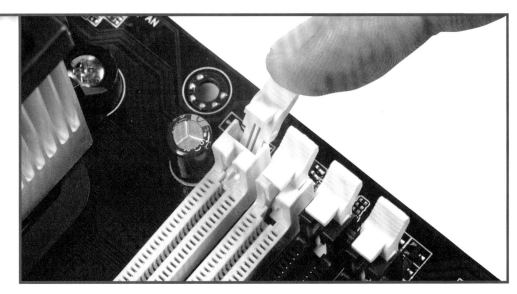

The memory slots and memory chips are shaped in such a way that you can't insert the chips backwards. Gently place the first memory module on the slot, ensuring that the connectors line up with the slot.

3

Push the memory module into the slot by pressing down from above. You'll need to exert a little bit of pressure to do this, but if the module doesn't appear to be going into the slot double-check that you haven't got it the wrong way round. If you have and you try to force the module into the slot, you could crack the motherboard.

4

When the module is in place the clips at the side of the slot should spring shut. If they don't, use a finger to close them. If they won't shut, the memory module isn't fully inserted.

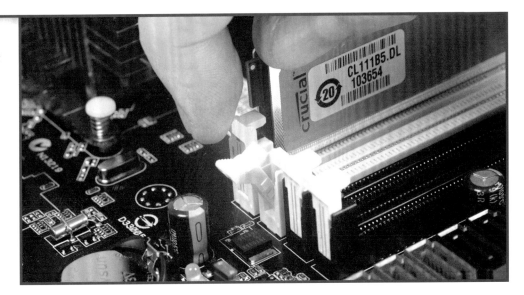

5

If you have a second memory module, repeat the process using the second yellow memory slot. Once the module is installed and the clips are holding it in place, put the motherboard to one side.

Installing the motherboard

We think it's much easier to install processors and memory modules when the motherboard isn't already in a case, but for everything else we need to have the motherboard in position. Every PC case is slightly different but the principles are the same. The most important thing is to ensure that the motherboard is screwed securely into position. With some cases, you may need to move the stand-offs, the little brass cylinders that you screw the motherboard into. Never try to force a motherboard into position: a little crack can cause serious damage.

Our Antec case is designed for easy access. The first thing to do is to remove the side panel. To do this, press the clip at the back of the case to unlock it and then push the side panel towards the front of the case.

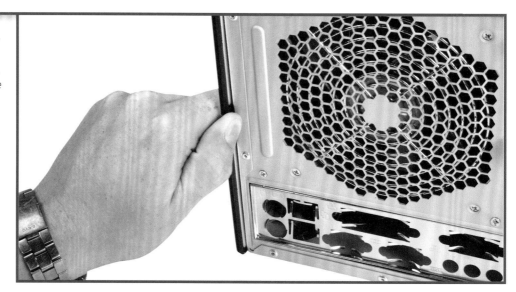

You should now be able to slide the panel off by pushing it forwards. If the panel doesn't move, try lifting the case up so that the panel isn't touching the table or worktop.

3

Now, remove the second side panel by following the same procedure. Remove any packaging or cables from inside the case and keep an eye out for a packet of screws. Most cases come with all the screws you'll need to install your various components.

4

Now, we need to remove the top of the case. With this model, the top of the case is secured with a single thumbscrew: simply unscrew it by hand, remove it and put it somewhere safe.

5

The top of the case should now lift off easily. With this particular design, the trick is to lift one edge and then slide the top off the case.

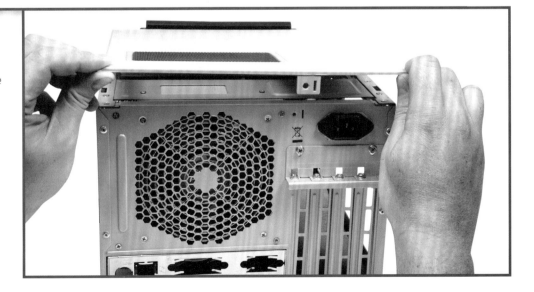

6

As you can see, this case is considerably smaller than the one we used for our first PC – but there's still plenty of room for all of our components. This particular case makes things easier by providing a removable drive cage, which enables you to install the DVD drive and hard disk separately.

7

The removable drive cage offers another benefit: we can take it out altogether to give us more working room. To do this, pull the cage towards the back of the case and then pull it upwards at around 45 degrees. This takes a little bit of force, so watch your fingers: the exposed edges of the case's innards can be sharp.

Pull the drive cage up and out to remove it, and then put it to one side. As you can see, we've now got considerably more room to work – which is handy, because the next bit is quite fiddly. Move the various cables inside the case out of the way as best you can.

At the back of the case you'll see a blanking plate, which is designed to leave room for the various connectors on your PC. This one is a generic one and won't fit the connections on our motherboard, so we need to remove it. We can't stress this enough: be very careful here. The metal is very thin and it's very easy to cut your fingers.

You'll find a replacement blanking plate supplied with your motherboard. The plate pops into the hole in the back of the case, but check it sits over your motherboard's connectors first: sometimes these plates are poorly machined, which means you'll need to clip off unwanted sections with a pair of pliers or tin snips to make them fit.

Your case will have a number of stand-offs – little bits of metal to which you screw your motherboard. If you're lucky, they'll already be in the correct places but, with some cases, you often find that you need to move them. The only way to check is to put the motherboard into the case, so we'll do that now.

Very carefully slide the motherboard inside the case and check that the holes in the motherboard match the positions of the stand-offs in the case. Make sure you don't scrape the motherboard on any part of the case as you move it into position. If the screw holes don't line up with the stand-offs, take the motherboard out and move the stand-offs.

When everything's lined up, make sure the blanking plate at the back is in the right position – it's impossible to adjust when the motherboard is screwed in place – and then screw the motherboard into position with the screws that came with the PC case. Don't overtighten the screws, as this can crack the motherboard.

PART **4**

Connecting the motherboard to the case

This section is nice and straightforward, but you might want to have the motherboard manual to hand as you connect the various bits and pieces: while motherboard manufacturers helpfully label every connection on the board, the labels are in very small print that's often very hard to read. Motherboard firms such as Asus provide clear diagrams in their manuals showing you exactly where the connectors are, which can save plenty of time and reduce eye strain.

You'll have noticed the spaghetti junction of cabling coming out of the power supply at the rear of the case. Locate the biggest power plug – it's a white block with 20 pins in it – and connect it to the power connector on the motherboard. On this motherboard, it's on the edge nearest the front of the case.

Now, locate the four-pin power block and connect it to the four-pin connector (here, it's just in front of the heatsink towards the right side of the case). The motherboard needs both power connectors to operate, so if you miss this step your PC won't boot, even if the other power connector is in place.

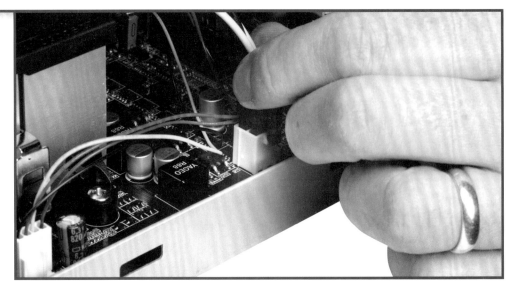

The next step is to connect the power supply's fan to the motherboard so your PC can control it. Locate the connector – with this particular case, it's the one with the blue and black wiring – and connect it to the PWR_FAN connector on the motherboard. Depending on the case there may be several fans to connect and it's essential that they're connected to the right bits of the motherboard.

Let's turn our attention to the cables on the front of the case. The first one we need is the POWER SWITCH cable which, as the label suggests, is for the power switch. Connect this to the PWR SWITCH connector on the motherboard.

We also need to connect the reset button. Locate the RESET SWITCH cable and connect it to the helpfully named RESET SWITCH connector.

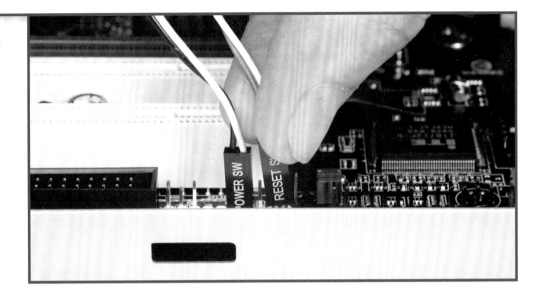

Depending on the case you have, you'll see a block marked HD AUDIO or AC97. This is for the case's audio inputs and outputs. Our case has both. HD AUDIO is the one we need here – it's for high-quality audio – so take this block and connect it to the HD AUDIO connector on the motherboard.

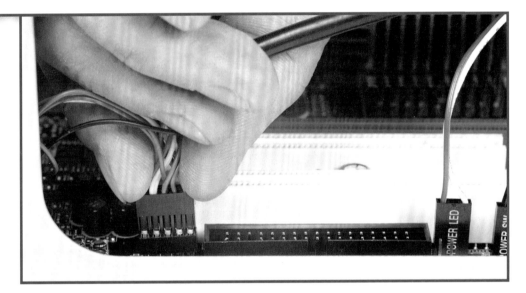

You should now be left with one more kind of connector, marked USB. This is for the USB ports on the front of the case and should be connected to the appropriate USB connector on the motherboard. You'll notice that the connector is marked to show what pins do what: it's important that you connect this plug the right way round. The motherboard manual shows the layout of the pins in the USB connectors so you can make sure the pins are connected correctly.

PART  Installing the hard disk and DVD drive

Remember the cage we took out earlier? It's time to get it back. Move the case to one side to make a bit of room and unpack the DVD and hard disk drives. You'll also need more of the screws that came with your case: neither the DVD nor the hard disk will include the necessary screws if you bought OEM versions (which you should, because they're cheaper).

To install the DVD drive, simply slide it into position in the space at the very top of the drive cage. This particular design is very clever: you can insert a 5-inch drive, such as a DVD player at the top, a 3.5-inch hard disk at the bottom, and a further two hard disks on either side (provided you haven't installed expansion cards in your PC that take up space).

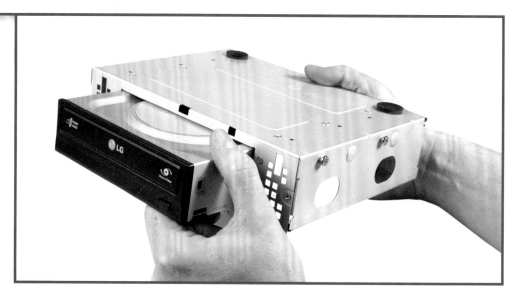

Now, take the hard disk and slide it into the smaller space immediately below the DVD drive. Make sure that the DVD drive and hard disk are situated with their connectors facing towards you – that is, towards the back of the case – or you won't be able to connect them to the motherboard.

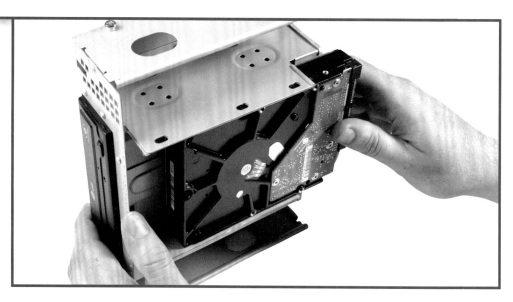

3

There are small screw holes on each side of the DVD drive. Line the holes up with the holes in the drive cage and screw the drive into position. Don't overtighten the screws. If you're determined to reduce noise, use screws with rubber washers: this can prevent the vibration from the drive being transmitted into the case. Screw the hard disk into position too.

4

Put the cage to one side and locate the SATA cables that came with your motherboard. There should be two: in the case of our Asus motherboard, they're bright pink for easy identification. Asus hasn't just colour coded the cables: it's colour coded the motherboard too. Look for the red SATA slots towards the front of the motherboard and connect a SATA cable to the first one. The connectors are shaped to ensure that they can't be connected the wrong way.

5

Now, connect the second SATA cable to the second red connector. Once you've done this, move the ends of the cables out of the way: it's time to put the drive cage into the case.

6

To install the drive cage, line up the pins in the cage with the slots in the case and lower the cage into position. When the cage is lowered there won't be enough room to get your hands in, so when you connect the various cables you'll need to lift the cage up slightly to make room for your fingers.

7

Connect the first SATA cable to the hard disk drive. As with the motherboard, the drive connectors are shaped so that you can't insert the SATA cable in the wrong way.

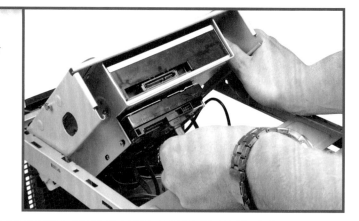

8

Now, connect the second SATA cable to the slot in the back of the DVD drive. Once again the cable and connector are L-shaped, so you cannot connect them the wrong way.

9

Locate one of the two SATA power cables that run from the power supply and connect it to the back of the DVD drive. As with the data connectors, both the cable and the connector are L-shaped.

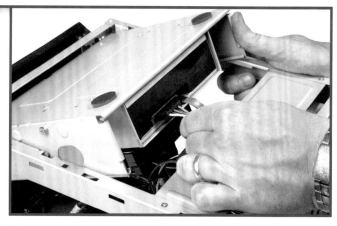

10

Now, connect the second SATA power connector to the hard disk drive. This is exceptionally fiddly as the power cables aren't very long. If you can't quite get the power cable to reach, loosen the screws that hold the hard disk in place, slide it slightly backwards and then screw it back into place when everything's connected.

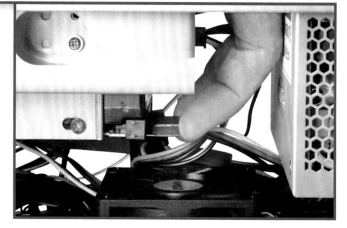

We're nearly finished: all we need to do now is put the case panels back on. Put the top panel on first, locking it into place with the thumbscrew.

Refitting the side panels is the reverse of removal: simply slide the panel on from the front and push it towards the back of the case until it locks into position. You'll find it much easier to do if you turn the case on its side.

Repeat the process for the second panel, ensuring that it locks into place. Give the case a quick check to ensure that the panels fit seamlessly. Congratulations! You've just built a small and surprisingly powerful PC. Now it's just a matter of connecting a keyboard, mouse and monitor and installing Windows.

TECHIE CORNER
Don't forget the disc!
Your motherboard's packaging will include a DVD or CD disc. You'll need this once you've installed Windows in order to get the correct drivers for the video, audio and network cards. Once you've used it, Windows will let you know about driver updates via Windows Update.

5

PART **Final touches**

We told you it was easy. All that remains now is to set up the computer to behave to your liking, install an operating system and finish off with a final expansion card. We will cover trouble-shooting in some detail, too, just in case of problems.

Connecting a monitor and switching on

At this point in the proceedings, you might be tempted to rush into further installations: the sound card, perhaps, or an internal modem or network card. However, now is the time to establish that everything has gone according to plan so far. Adding extra components merely complicates troubleshooting, should any be required.

With a monitor and keyboard connected, and optionally a mouse, give your new computer its first trial run.

Check it out

Give your work-in-progress a thorough once-over. Check that the heatsink and case fans are all still connected to the motherboard, that the memory modules are still clipped into their DIMMs, that the drives are all wired-up with ribbon and power cables, and that the video card is fully secured in its slot. You might like to reassemble the case now but it's not strictly necessary. You can even leave the case lying on its side to better monitor the action. However ... you will be working with live electricity from here on so never touch anything inside your PC's case while the PSU is connected to the mains power. Even when you turn off your computer, the PSU continues to draw power from the mains and the motherboard remains in a partially-powered standby state. We're only talking a 5V current, to be fair, but it's simply crazy to work on a 'live' motherboard or anything connected to it.

True, you could flip the PSU to Off (if it has its own power switch) and/or turn off the electricity at the wall socket (and hope that Junior doesn't turn it back on for a laugh while your head is buried in the case), but it's better and safer to get into the habit of always removing the power cable before conducting any internal work. This is the only cast-iron way to ensure no physical connection between yourself and the National Grid.

Booting up ... and down again

Connect the monitor to the video card's VGA or DVI port and plug it in to the mains. Turn on the monitor now. You might see a 'no signal' or similar message on the screen.

Now check that the PSU is set to the correct voltage – 220/230V in the UK – and connect it to the mains with your second power cable. Flip the PSU's power switch to the on position. Finally, press the on/off button on the front of the case. Your PC will come to life for the first time.

Look inside the case and check – by observation, not by touch – that the case fans are whirring. Don't worry if the heatsink fan isn't moving: modern processors and motherboards turn the heatsink fan on and off as required, so the heatsink might not need cooling when you first switch it on. If the case fan isn't working, however, kill the power immediately and check all the fan connections on the motherboard.

All being well, power your computer down with the on/off button and unplug the power cable. Leave the power switch on the PSU at the on position from now on. If all is not well, skip to p.148 now for some troubleshooting procedures.

Let us now turn our attention to some important configuration settings.

Once you're sure all your components are connected, you can put your PC's case back together.

FINAL TOUCHES

Essential system settings

The hard work is over, and you're nearly ready to use your brand new PC. However, before you can do that you need to know about two acronyms: POST and BIOS. POST stands for Power On Self Test and it tells you whether your PC is working properly. BIOS, pronounced 'bye-oss', is short for Basic Input and Output System and it tells your PC what bits are inside it and what to do with them.

When you switch on your PC, however, you might encounter a very small but very annoying problem: your keyboard isn't working. While modern motherboards come stuffed with USB ports and support USB keyboards, it's not unheard of for USB keyboard support to be turned off by default. If that's the case you'll need to go into the system BIOS and enable keyboard support – and to do that, you'll need a keyboard.

There are two solutions. You can beg or borrow an old, non-USB keyboard, or you can use a USB to PS/2 adapter. Whichever option you use, you can switch on your motherboard's USB keyboard support and then get rid of the old keyboard or the adapter.

Our photo shows a standard USB to PS/2 adapter, which fits

If your motherboard's USB support is turned off by default, you'll need one of these: it's a PS2 adapter that persuades your PC you have an old-style keyboard.

over the USB socket on your keyboard cable and enables you to plug it into the old-style PS/2 port on the back of the PC. If you're lucky, your USB keyboard will have come with such an adapter and you'll still have it; however if you're like us, you threw it out years ago. That means you'll have to nip to the supermarket to buy an ultra-cheap keyboard that includes the appropriate adapter.

Once you've installed the adapter or connected an old keyboard, it's time to switch on your PC and see what the POST has to say.

Beep codes
When you switch on your PC, you should hear a beep. What you're hearing is the result of the Power On Self Test, and if you

When you switch on your PC, you should see the splash screen. This is mainly an advert for the motherboard manufacturer, but it also tells you what keys to press if you want to access the BIOS setup.

have any major hardware problem you'll find out about it now. One beep is good, because it means that the POST hasn't found any problems. More than one beep isn't so good, because it means POST has found something bad.

The beep codes you hear will depend on which company created the BIOS, and you'll see their name on the screen that appears when you first power up your PC (provided, of course, that your video card is working). For example, if your motherboard uses a Phoenix BIOS and you hear one beep, then four beeps, then two beeps, POST is telling you that your memory isn't working; if you can't see anything on screen and you hear three beeps, then another three beeps, then four beeps, the motherboard can't find your video card. That might mean it isn't installed correctly or it could indicate that the video card is faulty. For advice on troubleshooting your PC, turn to p.148; for a full list of beep codes, turn to Appendix 3.

In most cases you'll hear a single, happy beep and the screen will display the 'splash page' that appears when you first boot your PC. This screen will tell you what key you need to press to enter the BIOS settings; in the case of our Gigabyte motherboard, we need to press <DEL> while the splash screen is displayed. If you don't press the appropriate key in time, don't worry; just reboot your PC and try again. After a few moments you should see your PC's BIOS and, while it looks quite scary, it's actually rather simple.

Changing BIOS settings

When the BIOS menu first appears you'll see some basic information on screen – typically, what keys you need to press to select menu options and edit their contents. What we're interested in, though, is the menu down the left hand side of the screen. Using the arrow keys, move the cursor until Standard Features is selected and then press Enter to go to that part of the BIOS menu.

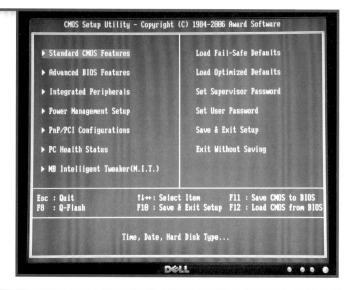

The Standard Features screen should now appear. There are two main things to check here: the system date and time; and the bits marked IDE Channel 0 Master and IDE Channel 1 Master. Your DVD drive and hard disk should appear in here; if they don't, then there's either a connection problem or one of the devices (or cables) is faulty. If everything's okay, just press ESC to return to the main BIOS menu.

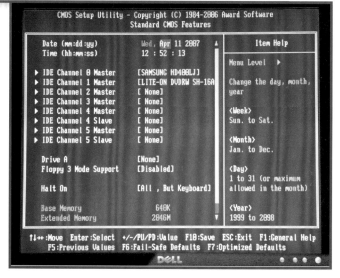

This time we want to go into the Advanced BIOS Features menu and adjust the boot order. The boot order is the order in which your PC looks at its various drives when you switch it on. For example, if you have a floppy disk drive as the first boot device, then your PC will look for an operating system on that when you switch it on. If it doesn't find it, you'll see an error message. With our PC we want to set our DVD drive as the first boot device and the hard disk as the second. There are several reasons for this. First, to install Windows we need to boot from the DVD drive; secondly, if we ever need to run a boot CD from our anti-virus software we need to boot it from the DVD drive before the PC turns to our hard disk. If your DVD drive isn't already the first boot device, change the order by pressing Enter to select the first boot device, using the arrow keys to select the DVD and then pressing Enter again to confirm the change. Press Esc when you've done this.

Now it's time to enable our USB keyboard. To do this, select Integrated Peripherals from the main menu. You should see two options – USB Keyboard and USB Mouse – and they're probably both set to 'Disabled'. We need to enable both options so we can use our USB keyboard and mouse with our PC.

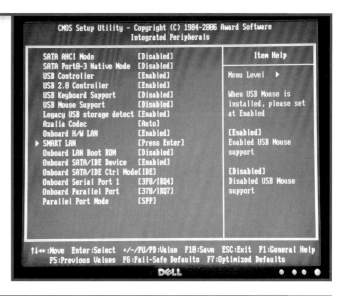

To enable USB support, use the arrow keys to select the appropriate option – in this case, USB Keyboard; some systems will call it Legacy USB Support or something similar – and press Enter. Now, use the arrow keys to select Enabled and press Enter again. That's the keyboard support turned on. Repeat the process for the USB Mouse option.

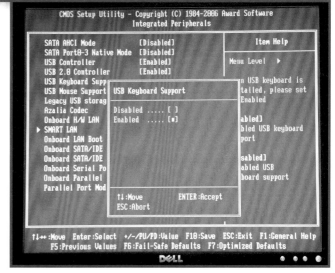

When you've turned on USB support, it's time to save your settings and exit. In our BIOS that means pressing the F10 key and selecting 'Yes' when the BIOS asks whether we really want to save and exit.

There's only one thing left to do now and that's to install the operating system.

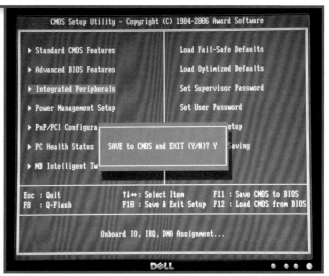

PART  # Installing Windows

Your lovingly assembled PC is ready to run, but you'll need to install an operating system before you can do anything useful with it. In this section, we'll discover which operating system to go for and how to get it up and running on your PC.

For our projects, we've chosen the OEM versions of Windows Vista Home Premium, with the 32-bit version for our full-sized PC and the 64-bit version for our smaller PC. We chose the OEM versions (which don't include manuals or technical support and can't be transferred to another PC) because they're significantly cheaper: £60 to £80, compared with retail prices of at least twice that amount.

Why did we choose a 32-bit version of Windows for one machine and a 64-bit version for the other? On paper, everyone should go for the 64-bit version because modern processors are 64-bit chips – so 64-bit Windows is the best option. In the real world, however, it's a bit more complicated than that. The reason we went for the 32-bit version on our main PC was compatibility: to use additional hardware (such as a TV tuner) with the 64-bit version of Windows, you need to install 64-bit drivers – and our chosen TV tuner card, the WinTV, didn't have 64-bit drivers available when we built our main PC. That wasn't an issue for our smaller PC, whose integrated sound and graphics systems already have 64-bit drivers. The other consideration with Windows is memory. The 32-bit version of Windows can't handle more than 4GB of memory, but the 64-bit version can. If you think you might end up putting more than 4GB of memory into your PC, then it's worth getting the 64-bit version, just in case.

Why Home Premium? Of all the versions of Windows Vista, we think Home Premium offers the best trade-off between price and power. It offers all the important goodies such as the Windows Aero user interface, but it's much cheaper than the all-singing, all-dancing Ultimate edition. However, as we'll discover in this section, it's possible to experiment with Ultimate even when you've bought a lesser version.

Before you decide on an OEM version of Vista rather than a boxed, retail copy, it's important to know the limitations of an OEM licence. The most important such limitation is that OEM versions are only available to system builders and they're designed to be installed on and sold with a brand new PC. That means OEM licences aren't transferable. When you buy a boxed retail copy of Vista you can move it from one PC to another – it isn't easy, but you can do it – but when you go for the OEM version, the licence has to stay with the PC. We don't think that's a problem because our PC is designed to last for years.

The second issue with OEM versions of Vista is that you don't get any documentation and you don't get technical support. That's why it's so cheap, but if you'd prefer a nice glossy manual and a phone number you can call for help then it might be worth buying a standard retail version. If, as for us, price is more important, we'd recommend the OEM option every time.

Finally, you can't buy OEM versions in the shops. However, most reputable online dealers such as Dabs.com will happily sell them to you provided you're also buying PC hardware.

Whether you go for the OEM version or the retail version of Vista, the installation process is the same – so how do you install Vista on your brand new PC? Let's find out.

TECHIE CORNER
What about Windows 7?
Windows 7 is the replacement for Windows Vista and Microsoft was due to start shipping it just after this edition went to print. The installation process is identical to that of Windows Vista and Home Premium is still the version to go for – so should you go for Windows 7 or Windows Vista?

The answer depends on what's important to you. The release of Windows 7 will inevitably mean that copies of Vista get even cheaper. While Vista suffered from various problems at launch (a few bugs, problems getting up-to-date device drivers), they've all been addressed. However, Windows 7 is slightly nicer than Vista and runs more quickly, especially on more modest hardware, so unless you're counting every last penny we think it makes sense to go for Windows 7. As with Vista, watch out for compatibility if you go for the 64-bit version: make sure there are 64-bit drivers for your graphics card, sound card or anything else you're putting in your PC before you buy a copy of Windows!

As you can see from the photograph, the OEM version of Windows Vista doesn't look very impressive: it's a dull cardboard box with lots of tiny text on it. You don't get a glossy manual or a nice box, but you do save more than £100 by going for the OEM version.

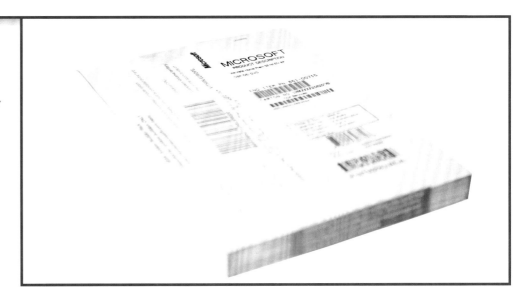

Inside the box you'll find a plastic DVD case. If your copy is legitimate, the DVD will be printed with a Microsoft hologram; if it isn't, don't go any further. Windows Vista uses a technology called Product Activation to spot dodgy copies, and after 30 days (or earlier if you try to activate Windows when you first run it) Microsoft will flip a kill switch that renders your copy of Vista unusable.

On the back of the DVD case, you'll see a label. Don't lose it: this contains your product key, and without it you won't be able to reinstall Windows at a later date. Once you've installed Vista it's a very good idea to affix the label to your PC's case, ideally in a place where it's easy to see if you need the product key in the future.

Installing Windows Vista is really very simple. Put the DVD in the drive, reboot your PC and after a bit of whirring the first installation screen will appear.

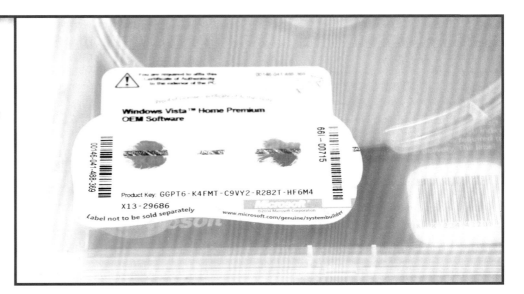

The first screen you'll see asks you to choose the language for your installation. Make sure that you choose the UK English and UK Keyboard options (assuming of course that you're in the UK and using a UK keyboard). If you select the US keyboard layout by mistake weird things will happen when you type, so for example instead of getting the @ symbol when you press the @ key, you'll get quotation marks instead.

⑤

This screen's straightforward enough: there's a great big button in the middle of the screen that says Install Now. Click it to continue.

⑥

The installer will now ask for your product key and there's also a tick box that says 'Activate Windows automatically when I'm online'. You can enter the key if you wish, but you don't need to do it right now – and if you don't, you can play with some interesting options, as we'll discover in the next screen.

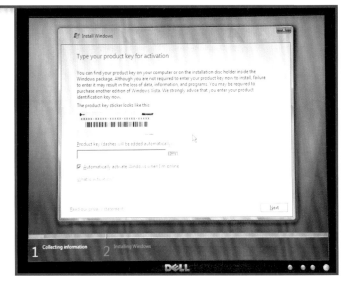

Every Windows Vista DVD includes every version of Windows Vista, so even though we've bought the Home Premium version the DVD also includes the (rubbish) Home Basic Edition and the (excellent but expensive) Ultimate Edition. If you wish, you can use this screen to install a different version of Vista than the one you've paid for and you've got 30 days to play with it before you need to activate Windows and stick with the version you actually own (alternatively you can use AnyTime Upgrade at this point, which is a Windows feature that enables you to upgrade the version you've got to a nicer, more expensive version; naturally, this costs money).

You won't see this screen if you've entered your product key in the previous step. That's because the product key tells the installer which version of Windows you've actually paid for. If you're curious there's no reason why you shouldn't install the Ultimate Edition rather than the Home Premium edition, although there's absolutely no point in trying a cut-down version such as Home Basic.

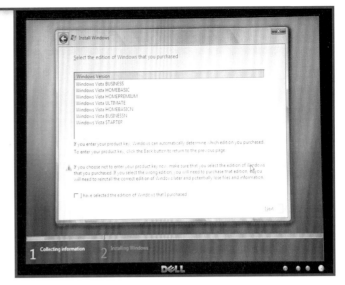

The next screen asks you to choose which kind of installation you want to perform, but in the case of OEM disks the choice is made for you and the 'upgrade' option is greyed out. That's because OEM versions are designed to be installed on a brand new PC that doesn't have an operating system to upgrade. The installer really, really wants you to click on the Advanced (Custom Install) option, and it would be impolite to disappoint it.

The installer will now ask where you want to install your copy of Windows Vista. Because we've installed a single, brand new hard disk there should be just one option here: unallocated space. That's the location we want to use, so click on Next to continue.

This would be a good time to make a cup of tea, because from now on the Windows Vista installer does everything automatically. Your PC will reboot a few times, the installer will show a few messages telling you how great Windows Vista is, and eventually the installation will finish. There are a few more steps we need to take before Vista is ready to use, but they're nice and quick.

When the installation is finished, you'll need to tell Windows
Vista what to call you. This is because files are stored under user
names and you can have several different people using the
same computer. You'll also be asked to choose a password. You
don't have to do this, but if your PC can be accessed by others
it's a very good idea. Click on next to continue.

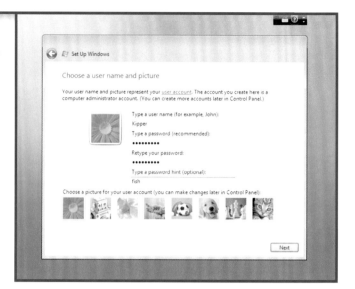

Now, the installer will ask you to give your computer a name.
This is for networking and it's the label your PC will have when
you're connecting to it from other networked PCs. You can't use
spaces or unusual characters, so you'll need to choose
something like JIM-PC here. You can also select a desktop
background here; the list is fairly short, but there's a much
bigger selection to choose from when you're actually using Vista.
Once again, click Next to continue.

You'll now be presented with three different security options.
99% of the time the first option, Use Recommended Settings, is
the one to go for. Unless you're already familiar with Windows
Vista and plan to tweak its security yourself, stick with the
recommended settings and then click on Next. The next screen
will ask you to choose a location for your computer. Click on
Home and then click Next.

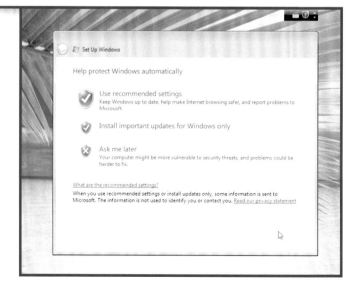

The next screen asks you to set the date and time, but they should already be correct – we set them in the BIOS a few minutes ago – so select the correct time zone, tick the 'automatically adjust clock' box and click on Next. You should now see the Thank You screen shown here. Click on the Start button and after a few seconds, the Windows Vista desktop will appear. You're finished!

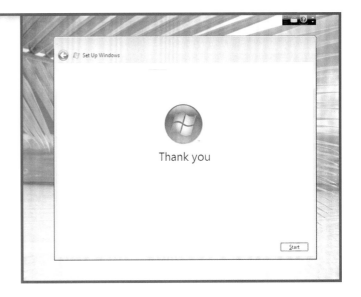

Here's the result of all your hard work and the odd cut finger: a brand-new, home-made PC running Windows Vista. This would be a good time to give yourself a pat on the back or to do a happy dance.

Driving you crazy

One of the first things Windows does is scan your system to see what hardware's in it. Windows then attempts to install the necessary device drivers that enable it to communicate with that hardware. However, you're likely to encounter a few problems – especially if your hardware choices are unusual. The first problem is that Windows Vista might not know what your hardware is and the second problem is that, even if it does correctly identify your hardware, it might not have the appropriate drivers.

One solution to the problem is to use the various CDs that came with your PC components. There'll be a CD with your motherboard, another one with your graphics card and so on. However, one thing we've encountered fairly frequently is that the drivers on those disks are for Windows XP and not Windows Vista, which uses a completely different kind of driver technology. If that's the case with your hardware, you'll need to turn to the internet. For example, to get the most up-to-date drivers for our graphics card we had to visit the support section of the ATI website. Doing this is a major pain in the neck, but it's worth doing in order to get a stable system.

Most Windows Vista problems of the 'my screen isn't working properly', 'everything looks funny' and 'I can't select a high resolution' variety are the result of old or incorrect driver software. For example, if you can't persuade Windows to display the snazzy Aero Glass interface that's usually a driver fault. Installing up-to-date drivers and restarting your system usually solves the problem.

QUICK Q&A

Now what?
Windows Vista comes with some security software: Windows Defender, which tries to stop spyware from sneaking onto your system, and Windows Firewall, which blocks potentially malicious programs from connecting to your PC (if they're not yet on your system) or connecting to the internet (if they are on your system). However, we'd strongly recommend investing in a serious anti-virus program too. We've had good results with BitDefender AntiVirus and Panda AntiVirus programs, but there are lots to choose from.

When you first run Windows Vista, it's a very good idea to run Windows Update (Start > All Programs > Windows Update) to download the latest patches for your system.

Moving Vista from another PC

If the computer you're building is designed to replace another machine that's already running Windows Vista and you still have the installation disc, you can move that copy of Vista to your new computer provided that it isn't an OEM version (which is locked to the first machine you install it on – the licence terms prohibit you from moving it to a different PC). However, while the installation process is the same as with any other copy of Vista, once you've got your machine up and running you'll encounter an irritating problem.

When you try to activate Windows on your new machine, you'll get a message telling you that your product key has already been used. Don't despair, though: the activation screen gives you a phone number to call and if you're patient, you'll eventually be able to speak to someone who will deactivate the old product code (rendering the copy of Vista on your old PC redundant) and give you a brand new activation code for your new PC.

Installing a sound card

If you are not content with integrated audio or if your motherboard lacks such capability, you'll want to install a sound card. This can be installed in any PCI expansion slot. First, though, revisit the BIOS menu and disable the onboard audio chip.

You can disable your motherboard's integrated audio chip in the BIOS menu. Do this before installing a sound card. If you leave the setting on Auto, the motherboard should recognise the presence of a new card and turn off integrated audio automatically – but there's no guarantee.

Turn off your computer, unplug it from the mains and take the usual antistatic precautions. Open the computer case and lay it on its side. Now familiarise yourself with the layout of the expansion card (i.e. read the manual), decide which PCI slot to use and remove the corresponding blanking plate from the case. Remove the card from its antistatic bag and carefully install it in the expansion slot. Be sure not to touch any components. Secure the card to the case chassis with the screw.

Now connect the audio cables from your CD/DVD drives – but see p.139 first.

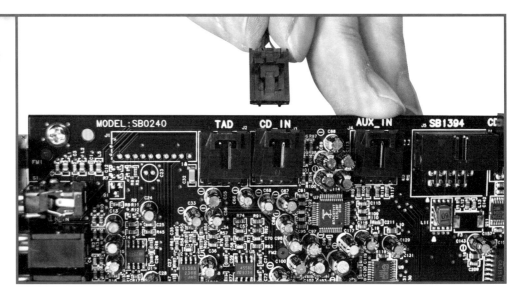

This card is supplied with an optional port bracket that supplies the computer with a MIDI/games port. It connects to the sound card by means of a cable. Note that a port bracket effectively blocks an expansion slot so you may prefer to live without one if slots are in short supply. With a small form factor case, you probably won't have the option to use a port bracket.

Remove a blanking plate and screw the port bracket into position next to the sound card. Finally, replace the computer covers, plug it in and fire it up. Windows will identify the new component and ask for a driver. Pop the supplied CD-ROM in the drive and follow the directions. You should also install any applications software shipped with the card and, of course, connect your speakers.

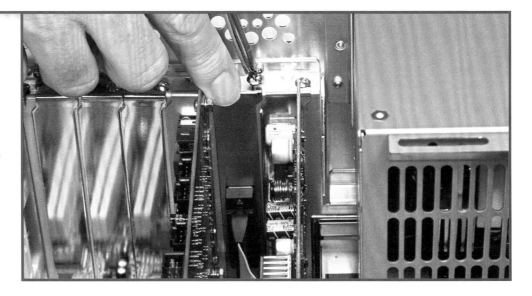

PART 5 Digital audio extraction

We mentioned earlier (p.61) that many drives support
digital audio extraction (DAE). With speakers connected
to the sound card, this is the time to find out.

First, establish that you can hear an audio CD when played in
the CD/DVD drive. Then check that DAE has been enabled within
Windows. In Windows XP, click Start, Control Panel, Performance
& Maintenance and System. This launches the System Properties
window. Look in the Hardware tab and click Device Manager.
Here you will find a list of all the hardware devices in your
computer. Click the little '+' sign next to DVD/CD-ROM drives
and then double-click the drive in question. In the Properties tab,
ensure that the 'Enable digital CD audio for this CD-ROM device'
box is checked (ticked). If this option is greyed-out and
unclickable, the drive does not support DAE and you'll definitely
need to use an audio cable. Repeat with the DVD drive.

In Windows Vista, the easiest way to check everything's
connected properly is to click Start > Windows Media Player and
then click on the arrow below the Rip button. Choose More
Options from the menu and a dialog box will appear. Click on the
Devices tab, select your drive and then click on Properties. If
everything's connected you should see 'Digital' selected in both
the Playback and Rip sections.

Now turn off your computer, remove the covers and disconnect
the audio cable from either the drive or the sound card. Reboot
and try playing the CD again. If you still hear sound, you know
that the drive supports DAE and you can remove the cable
altogether.

Alternatively, of course, you can opt not to bother with internal
audio cables in the first place and take a chance that DAE will
work. That's what we do.

QUICK Q&A

**How many PCI cards can I
install?**
As many as you have slots for on
your motherboard. The PCI bus is
natively 'Plug-and-Play', which
means the computer can apportion
system resources automatically
and avoid hardware conflicts.

It's not such a huge deal, really,
but Digital Audio Extraction lets
you dispense with those fiddly
internal sound cables. Anything
that reduces the risk of cables
snagging fans is welcome.

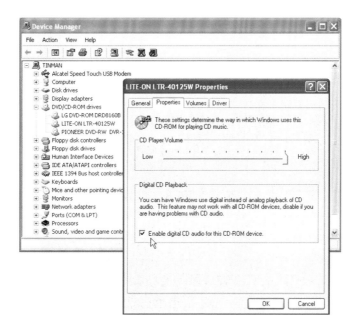

Loose ends

You should now have a fully-functioning, home-built, better-than-off-the-shelf PC at your disposal. Congratulations – the hard work is done! If everything is behaving as it should, now is the time to consider further hardware installations to complete the picture.

In a mid-tower case such as this it's not always easy to clear away extraneous clutter. Just ensure that cables are kept well away from fans and check that airflow in and out of the case is not blocked. Here, the sound card's bracket cable is rather too close to the video card's heatsink.

There is one final, rather pressing matter to take care of, namely tidying your PC's interior. The trouble here is that there's no 'right' way to do it as such; it's really just a matter of bunching together surplus power cables and tucking them out of the way … somewhere. A free drive bay is fine. Keep dangling cables away from fans and other components, and ensure that, so far as possible, cables do not impede airflow through the case. Your computer case manufacturer may have included a few plastic cable ties, or else you can use your own. Avoid metal ties, even if coated in paper or plastic, as these could short-circuit the motherboard. Again, the benefits of a tall tower case with plenty of room are apparent, but even a mid- or mini-tower can be kept reasonably tidy.

A full-tower case is a cinch to keep tidy. This example is further helped by the use of round IDE/ATA cables instead of the usual flat ribbon cables and a side-mounted hard disk drive.

Free software

You've blown the budget on your PC components, but don't despair: even if you've spent all your cash, you can still get seriously good software for your new PC.

Before you start looking for software, though, it's worth looking at Windows Vista itself. For example, the Home Premium edition we've chosen includes all of the following software:

- A decent web browser
- A good email client
- Security (firewall and anti-spyware)
- Photo organising and editing
- Windows Media Player for music, DVD and movies
- Media Center software that turns your PC into a complete entertainment centre
- Integrated CD and DVD burning
- Movie editing and DVD creation
- Scheduled file backup
- Games, including 3D chess

In some cases, you might also get software with the components you've bought. For example, our DVD drive came with a free copy of the excellent WinDVD playback software and some graphics cards come with free games. However, no matter what's inside Vista or what goodies you got with your PC components, the one thing you won't have is an Office suite.

Office suites take care of word processing, spreadsheets and so on. As with Windows Vista, you can get OEM versions of Microsoft Office 2007 at a reasonable price – at the time of writing, the OEM version of Office 2007 Home and Student Edition is around £75, compared to around £100 for the non-OEM edition – but, before you spend more money, it's a good idea to check out some of the alternatives. Thanks to Open Source software, it's possible to get a very good rival to Office for free.

The Home Premium and Ultimate editions of Windows Vista are stuffed with software, including DVD creation and even media center software.

The cheapest version of Microsoft Office 2007 is the Home and Student Edition, which costs around £75 in OEM form – but OpenOffice.org offers similar features for free.

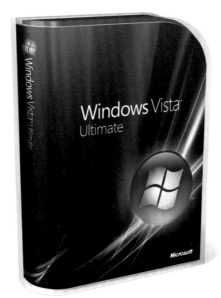

Introducing OpenOffice.org

OpenOffice.org is a very credible rival to Microsoft Office. It can read and write Office documents and it can do most of the things the various parts of Microsoft Office can do – but it's completely free. There's even a portable version that you can download and put on a USB pen drive, which means you can take the entire suite wherever you go and run it on any computer you like. If you've got broadband you can download it for free from **http://download.openoffice.org**, although we wouldn't recommend doing it on a dial-up modem connection: the Windows download is a mighty 106MB.

So what do you get for no money? There are six programs in the OpenOffice.org suite: Writer, for word processing; Impress, for presentations; Math, for mathematical calculations; Draw, for creating and editing images; Calc, for spreadsheet work; and Base, for managing databases. For most people Writer and Calc are where you'll spend most of your time.

OpenOffice.org looks very similar to Microsoft Office, so you don't need to worry about learning a whole new way of doing things. There are a few differences – things you'd expect to find under one menu appearing under another one, the odd button appearing in a different place and so on – but there's nothing too dramatic, and OpenOffice.org is a nice place to spend time in. It's also very powerful, and like Microsoft Office it's ideal for beginners and advanced users alike. However, as with most Office-a-likes don't be surprised if you encounter the odd problem

The open source package OpenOffice.org looks like Office and works like Office, but it won't cost you a penny.

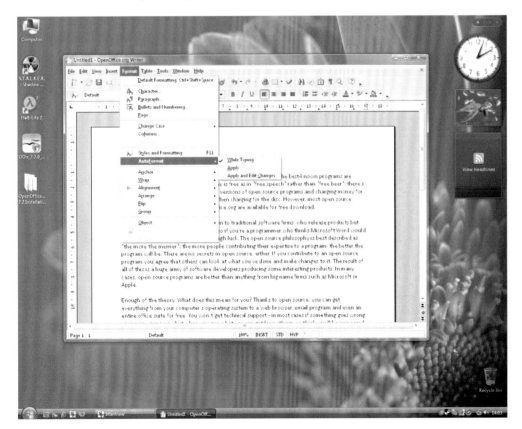

when you try to import very complicated files created in Word and Excel, and if presentation software is a key requirement then you might find the Impress program less impressive than rival products.

You can even make OpenOffice.org save in Microsoft Office-compatible file formats by default. To do this in Writer, for example, go to Tools > Options > Load/Save > General and choose the Microsoft Word 97/2000/XP option. From now on, every document you save in Writer will be in Microsoft Word format.

For most jobs, OpenOffice.org is very impressive but there is one key issue that you might want to consider. When you use most software there's a technical support department you can call; with OpenOffice.org, there isn't. You can find answers to most questions on the internet, but if you want the reassurance of knowing that you can telephone an expert when things go wrong, then OpenOffice isn't for you.

So how can OpenOffice.org give you a fully featured office suite for free? The reason is a philosophy called Open Source, which is responsible for producing lots of high-quality software and then giving it away for nothing. See the Techie Corner box below for more about the Open Source philosophy.

Other essentials

Anti-Virus software Although Windows Vista includes some security software – a firewall to block nasties, and a program called

TECHIE CORNER

Free as a bird

Open Source is all about free software. However, while most of the best-known programs are indeed free, the movement's philosophy is free as in 'free speech' rather than 'free beer': there's nothing to stop firms making their own versions of open source programs and charging money for them, or offering programs on CD and then charging for the disc. However, most open source software, such as the excellent OpenOffice.org, are available for free download.

The open source movement is a reaction to traditional software firms, who release products but prohibit you from fiddling with them – so if you're a programmer who thinks Microsoft Word would be better if you did some tweaking, tough luck. The open source philosophy is best described as 'the more the merrier': the more people contributing their expertise to a program, the better the program will be. There are no secrets in open source, either. If you contribute to an open source program, you agree that others can look at what you've done and make changes to it. The result of all of this is a huge army of software developers producing some interesting products. In many cases, open source programs are better than anything from big name firms such as Microsoft or Apple.

Enough of the theory. What does this mean for you? Thanks to open source, you can get everything from your computer's operating system to a web browser, email program and even an entire office suite for free. You won't get technical support – in most cases if something goes wrong you're on your own – but when you see what you can get for nothing, we think you'll be impressed.

Google Docs & Spreadsheets provides basic word processing, spreadsheet and presentation features, and it all happens inside your Web browser.

Windows Defender to spot malicious software – it doesn't have any anti-virus protection. Such software is essential when you're using the internet, but the good news is that you can get it for free.

There are several free anti-virus programs for Windows including AVG Anti-Virus (**http://free.grisoft.com**), AVAST Home Edition (**www.avast.com**) and the open source ClamWin (**www.clamwin.com**). Of the three, we like AVG and AVAST best, not least because at the time of writing ClamWin hadn't been updated to support Windows Vista. Both programs are free for non-commercial use, so if you use your PC for work then you'll need to pay for a commercial licence or look at a paid-for alternative product.

Multi-chat software Although Vista includes Windows Live Messenger, an excellent chat program, it's not a great deal of help if your friends or colleagues use a rival chat system. A multi-chat client, such as the excellent Trillian (**www.trillian.cc**), solves the problem by connecting to all the major chat networks and enabling you to communicate without running a different program for each network.

Online offices

The programs we've looked at so far all have one thing in common: to use them, you need to install them on your PC. However, a new breed of programs works in a very different way; instead of installing them you simply access them through your Web browser. You can use word processing software, spreadsheet software, email software, calendar software … if you can imagine it, there's probably a website that offers it. Even better, most such sites are free.

One of the best-known online suites is Google Docs &

Spreadsheets (**http://docs.google.com**), which provides an excellent word processor, spreadsheet and, soon, a presentation package inside your web browser. The programs are all free (although there are paid-for versions that provide you with extra storage) and work very well, and while they're not as powerful as OpenOffice.org they're not supposed to be. If all you need to do is bash out the odd letter or analyse a few figures, Google Docs & Spreadsheets will do the job quite happily.

Google isn't the only firm offering free, online software. Lots of sites offer online word processing and spreadsheet software, and some of the computer industry's biggest names are getting in on the act too. For example Adobe, whose Photoshop is the king of image-editing software, has announced its plans for a free, cut-down version of Photoshop Elements that you'll be able to access from any web browser.

Provided you have a broadband connection – dial-up modem connections just aren't fast enough – there are several key benefits to web-based software. In most cases, traditional software costs a great deal of money, but most online applications are free. They're also updated immediately, so if they need a security fix or a bug fix you don't need to download it. Instead, the next time you access the program you'll automatically use an updated version. Finally, many online programs enable you to store documents online, which means you can work from anywhere you can get internet access instead of having to carry your documents around with you on a USB flash drive or a CD-R.

Web wobbles

For all the benefits of using web-based programs, there are plenty of negatives too:

It's only as fast as your internet connection Online applications depend on computers that may be hundreds or even thousands of miles away, and if the connections between you and those computers are congested then the performance of the program will deteriorate dramatically.

No connection, no software In most cases, you can't access online software if you can't get online. Some services such as Google Docs enable you to work in offline mode when you're not connected to the internet, but if all your files are on Google's computer you won't be able to access them until you get back online.

It might not always be available We're big fans of online email systems such as Google Mail (**http://mail.google.com**), but we regularly encounter periods when the service isn't available – which means our email isn't available either. Other online services suffer from the same problems, so for example you might find that when you try to access the service to do something important it's 'temporarily unavailable' due to 'scheduled maintenance'.

It might not be very good Some online services – Google Mail, the 30boxes calendar system (**http://30boxes.com**) and so on – are very good. However, some online services aren't. For example, ajaxWrite (**www.ajaxwrite.com**) was launched amid claims that 'for 90% of the people in the world, the need to buy Microsoft Word just vanished' but, in our experience, it's very basic, very slow, prone to crashing and it doesn't work in internet

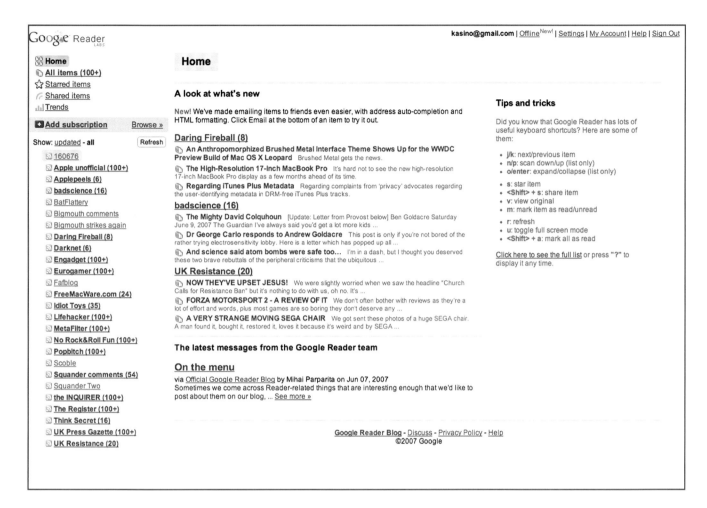

Explorer. It's a similar story with the online graphics program ajaxSketch (**www.ajaxsketch.com**), which has been described as an alternative to high-end graphics programs such as Adobe Illustrator. It's nothing of the sort.

There's no technical support With traditional software, there's usually a helpline you can call if you encounter trouble. With web-based software, there isn't.

If the site disappears, so does the software Google isn't likely to disappear any time soon, but what about the other online services? There are lots of me-too applications, for example, in the world of online word processors and spreadsheets there are dozens of sites offering essentially the same kinds of software. Inevitably some of those sites won't last, and if you choose one of the ones that doesn't last the course then there's always the risk that it'll disappear overnight and take the software – and your documents – with it.

It might not be free forever Most online applications are free, especially the ones labelled 'beta' (more of that in a moment). However, there's no way to predict whether a particular program will stay free forever, or whether it'll cost money at a later date. If you come to depend on a particular program and the developers decide to charge for it, you'll either have to pay up or spend lots of time moving your data to an alternative program.

Although most web applications need an internet connection, a growing number can be used when you're not connected. Google Reader's newsreading program is one such package.

It's usually in beta If – like most online applications we've seen – a program is labelled as a 'beta' or a 'preview', that means it isn't finished. 'Beta' is computer industry shorthand for 'help us find the bugs', and it's generally accepted that beta software might do strange things, crash your computer or even destroy your data. That's fine if you want to experiment with cutting-edge technology, but if you use beta software (whether it's online or on your computer) for business-critical tasks then you're taking a very big risk.

Web-based services are improving quickly and in a few years, they could well be a better option than traditional programs. For basic Office tasks they're well worth considering, but for heavyweight jobs we'd stick with traditional software, whether that's a big-name package such as Microsoft Office or an open source alternative such as OpenOffice.org.

Troubleshooting

Let's assume you've built your PC, turned it on for the first time ... and nothing happens. You can't get into BIOS, let alone install Windows. How and where do you begin to troubleshoot?

In fact, identifying a problem at this stage is very much easier than down the road when you've got a printer, scanner, webcam and goodness knows what other hardware attached; not to mention 57 software programs doing their utmost to interfere with one another, a real risk of viruses and perhaps a utility suite that does more harm than good. Your computer will never be so easy to diagnose and cure as it is right now.

Check the cables

The very first step is all too obvious but all too often overlooked: check that all external cables are securely connected in the correct places:

- ☐ The computer's PSU should be plugged into a mains wall socket (or power gangplank).

- ☐ So should the monitor.

- ☐ The mains electricity supply should be turned on at the wall.

- ☐ The monitor should be connected to the video card's VGA or DVI output.

- ☐ The keyboard should be connected to the computer's PS/2-style keyboard port (not to a USB port, unless USB support has already been enabled in BIOS, and not to the mouse port).

- ☐ The PSU should be set to the correct voltage and turned on.

Now turn on the monitor. A power indication LED on the monitor housing should illuminate and, hopefully, you'll see something on the screen. If not, re-read the monitor manual and double-check that you've correctly identified the on/off switch and are not busy fiddling with the brightness or contrast controls. It's not always obvious which switch is which. If the power light still does not come on, it sounds like the monitor itself may be at fault. Try changing the fuse in the cable. Ideally, test the monitor with another PC.

Internal inspection

Now turn on the PC itself. Press the large on/off switch on the front of the case, not the smaller reset switch. You should hear the whirring of internal fans and either a single or a sequence of beeps. But let's assume that all seems lifeless. Again, check/change the fuse in the PSU power cable. If this doesn't help, unplug all cables, including the monitor, take off the case covers and lay the computer on its side. Now systematically check every internal connection. Again, here's a quick checklist to tick off:

- ☐ The PSU should be connected to the motherboard with a large 24-pin plug and also, if appropriate, with ATX 12V and ATX Auxiliary cables.
- ☐ The heatsink fan should be plugged into a power socket on the motherboard.
- ☐ The case fans should be likewise connected.
- ☐ All drives should be connected to the appropriate sockets on the motherboard with ribbon cables.
- ☐ All drives should be connected to the PSU with power cables.
- ☐ The video card should be securely sited in its AGP or PCI Express slot.
- ☐ All other expansion cards should be likewise in place.
- ☐ Look for loose screws inside the case, lest one should be causing a short-circuit.
- ☐ If your motherboard has jumpers, check that they are correctly set.
- ☐ Check the front panel connections. If the case's on/off switch is disconnected from the motherboard, you won't be able to start the system.
- ☐ Are any cables snagging on fans?
- ☐ Double-check that Pin 1 positions on cables and drives are correctly matched (confession time: we initially got this wrong with the un-keyed floppy drive cable plug).
- ☐ Are the retention clips on the memory DIMMs fully closed?
- ☐ Does anything on the motherboard look obviously broken or damaged?

Disconnect each cable in turn and look for bent pins on the plugs and sockets. These can usually be straightened with small, pointy pliers and a steady hand. Reconnect everything, including the monitor and power cable, and turn the computer on once more. Leave the covers off to aid observation. Does it now burst into life as if by magic? Rather gallingly, unplugging and replacing a cable is sometimes all it takes to fix an elusive but strictly temporary glitch.

PSU problems

Look for an LED on the motherboard (check the manual for its location). This should illuminate whenever the PSU is connected to the mains power and turned on, even when the computer itself is off. The LED confirms that the motherboard is receiving power; if it stays dark, the PSU itself may be at fault.

When you turn on the computer, do the fans remain static? Does the CD drive disc tray refuse to open? Is all depressingly dead? This would confirm the PSU as the problem. Use an alternative power cable, perhaps borrowed from the monitor, just to be sure. If still nothing happens, remove and replace the PSU.

NEVER TRY TO OPEN OR REPAIR A PSU. Nor should you try running it while it's disconnected from the motherboard, as a PSU can only operate with a load.

Next steps

Let's assume that there is evidence of power flowing to the motherboard: the LED comes on and the heatsink and case fans spin. The PSU must be okay but there's still nothing on the monitor screen. Did you hear a beep as the computer powered up? This is a good thing. A sequence of beeps is generally a sign – a welcome sign, in fact – of specific, identifiable trouble. See the Power On Self Test (POST) section on p.151.

Check the keyboard. If anything is resting on the keys, remove it. This alone can cause a computer to pause. As the computer powers up, three lights on the keyboard should illuminate within the first few seconds. If they fail to do so, it's just possible that a dud keyboard is responsible for halting the entire system. Disconnect it and reboot the computer without a keyboard attached. If you now see a keyboard error message on the monitor screen where all was blank before, it looks like you need a new one. Connect an alternative keyboard to the computer and reboot again to confirm the diagnosis.

Another clue: if the computer partially boots but then stalls, check the memory count during the POST procedure. If the RAM total differs from the memory you installed, it looks like you have a DIMM problem to deal with. Remove, clean and replace each module. If that gets you nowhere, try booting with a single module in place, and experiment with each in turn. Check the motherboard manual for details here; a single module must usually be installed in a specific DIMM slot (usually DIMM1). If you can start the computer successfully at some point, you should be able to identify and exclude faulty modules. This isn't much help if you only have one module, of course.

Back to basics

Failing all of the above, disconnect all power and ribbon cables from the drives and the motherboard. Unplug and remove the video card and any other expansion cards, disconnect the case fans and leave only a single memory module in place. In short, reduce the system to a bare bones configuration where the only remaining connections are between the PSU and the motherboard: ATX power, ATA Auxiliary and ATX 12V. Do not

When handling expansion cards, be very careful not to touch either their onboard components or the lower gold connecting edge. With a card out of its slot, take the opportunity to clean its connecting edge with a lint-free cloth.

remove the heatsink or processor and leave all the front panel connections in place.

Now turn on the power once more. You should hear some diagnostic beeps from the BIOS. If so, see the following POST section and Appendix 3. If not, check the speaker connection.

If that doesn't resolve matters, turn off the computer, remove the power cable, and gradually, carefully, step-by-step, put it all back together again. Begin with the video card. Connect a monitor you know to be working and reboot the system. This will give you the added benefit of being able to read any onscreen error messages as you go along. If the screen stays blank, you know for sure that the video card is at fault. Replace it.

Reconnect a functioning keyboard next. Reboot and check that your computer gets past POST – i.e. that you can successfully enter the BIOS Setup routine. Now reconnect the floppy drive ribbon and power cables and reboot once more. Reinstall the hard disk drive next, followed by the CD and DVD drives. Every step of the way, reboot the computer and ensure that it doesn't hang or abort during POST. At some point, the computer may refuse to start – and right there you will have identified your problem. Alternatively, it may start normally all the way through and you may never find out what the original stumbling block was. No matter: either way, you have successfully solved your hardware hassles.

Power On Self Test (POST)

The very first thing a computer does when it starts is give itself a quick once-over to check that it still has a processor, memory and motherboard. If this POST procedure finds a serious problem, or 'fatal error', it is likely to throw a wobbly and halt the computer in its tracks. That's the assumption we have been working on in this section.

However, it also gives you two useful diagnostic clues (actually three, but hexadecimal checkpoint codes are beyond the scope of this book).

First, assuming that the video card and monitor are both working, you should see some onscreen error messages. These may be self-explanatory or relatively obscure, depending on the problem and the BIOS manufacturer, but should offer at least some help. A memory error would indicate that one or more of your modules is either faulty or not properly installed; a 'hard disk not found' message would most likely point to a loose connection or perhaps a faulty IDE/ATA cable.

Secondly, so long as the case speaker is connected, the motherboard will emit a series of POST-generated beeps. These can help you identify the specific component causing the problem.

We list some common beep code and error messages in Appendix 3.

POST is a low-key but essential routine that the computer runs through before launching Windows or any other operating system. Keep an eye out for error messages on the screen and an ear out for beep codes.

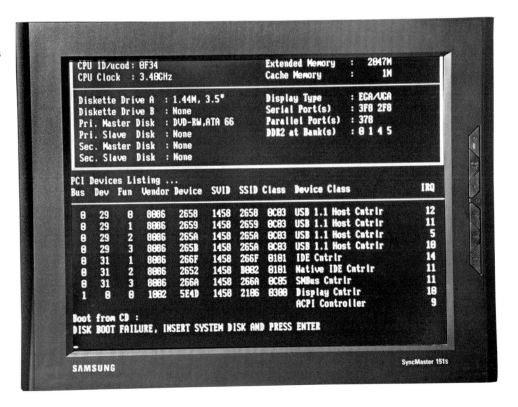

PART **6**

Appendices

PART

Appendix 1
Silence is golden ... well, copper and aluminium

If there is one thing the average desktop computer is not, it is quiet. Gallingly, the more high-powered you make it, the noisier it becomes. It all boils down to the cooling systems inside the case, i.e. a bunch of low-tech fans. There are fans in the PSU, fans built into the case, a fan on the processor heatsink, probably another on the Northbridge chip and yet another on the video card. Combined, they make a racket that's loud enough to be off-putting at best and to drown out music or game soundtracks at worst.

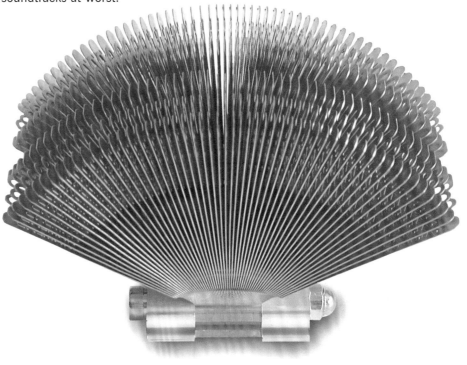

Freaky-looking it may be but this completely-silent Zalman 'Flower Cooler' can replace a boisterous CPU heatsink. All it needs is a really big, really quiet fan to supply it with fresh air.

However, there are some useful counter-measures available and here the DIY system builder can customise a computer to suit. For one, consider a passive heatsink for the processor, i.e. one without a powered fan. There are plenty of bizarre-looking but highly-effective heatsinks around that can keep the processor well within acceptable temperature limitations (under 75° Celsius for a Pentium 4).

Even chipset fans tend to be irritatingly intrusive, so you might care to remove the Northbridge heatsink and replace it with a silent fan-less alternative.

Most recent video cards also use fan-assisted heatsinks to cool the GPU. Here again it is often possible to replace the original with a silent version. Be careful, though: some of the latest video chips run so hot that a passive heatsink alone is not sufficient unless there is also a fan nearby to supply cool air.

There's little to do about a noisy PSU other than replace it with a quiet one – or, of course, to buy a quiet PSU in the first place. Check the specs and look for an acoustic noise level of about 30dB when the unit is running at 75% capacity.

Going further, you can even encase the hard disk drive in an acoustic enclosure and clad the interior of the case with sound-muffling panels.

Cooling caveats

Just a couple:

1. In smaller cases, the PSU is often located directly above the processor socket (as, in fact, in our project – see p.92). This generally rules out a passive heatsink because there simply isn't the necessary clearance over the processor. And even if you can squeeze one into the available space, don't forget that …

2. Even an elaborate super-effective passive heatsink needs some independent cooling. This is generally provided by a large, variable-speed ultra-quiet fan positioned directly above the heatsink and held in place with an angled bracket attached to the case. Again, this is not possible in most mid-tower cases.

In short, don't shell out for an inventive cooling solution unless you're sure your case can accommodate it. If you have an unobstructed view of the processor socket when the motherboard and PSU are both in place inside the case, you should be OK.

Consult Quiet PC for specialist advice and products, including the Zalman range of silent heatsinks (see Appendix 4).

If your chipset has a fan, consider replacing it with an efficient passive heatsink. So long as there is reasonable airflow inside the case, this will keep it cool and quiet.

If even the clicking of the hard disk drive drives you to distraction, encase your case in mufflers.

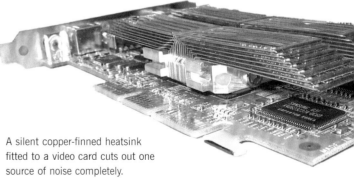

A silent copper-finned heatsink fitted to a video card cuts out one source of noise completely.

Appendix 2
That's entertainment: making a media centre PC

If your PC lives in a spare bedroom you might not be using its full potential: these days even the humblest PC is an entertainment powerhouse. So why not put it in the living room?

The computer you've built with the help of this book isn't just a powerful business and gaming machine. With the right software, a couple of components and a few simple tweaks it can be an all-singing, all-dancing multimedia marvel, so it's a shame to keep it tucked away in a spare bedroom or the study.

If like us you plumped for the Home Premium edition of Windows Vista, all the software you need is already sitting on your PC – and if you also installed a TV tuner card, all the hardware you need is there too.

Here's what your PC can do:

- It's a fully featured DVD player and you can connect your sound card to your stereo for stunning soundtracks.
- It's a digital jukebox that can store all your music and even your music videos, playing them through your TV or your hi-fi.
- It's a CD maker that you can use to burn your own compilation CDs.
- It's a movie marvel that can import and edit movies and then publish them to DVD.
- It's a showcase for your digital photos with special effects, videos and slideshows.

This is an off-the-shelf Media Center PC but you can just as easily build your own. Note the digital TV tuner card, which is all you need to receive Freeview channels.

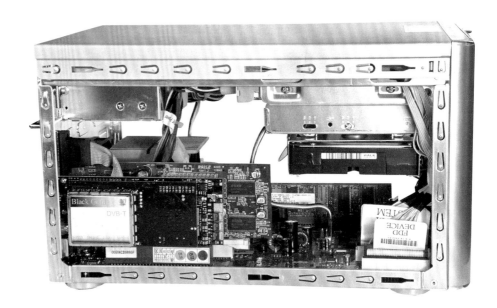

The Home Premium and Ultimate editions of Windows Vista include Media Center, which is designed to turn your PC into a multimedia marvel.

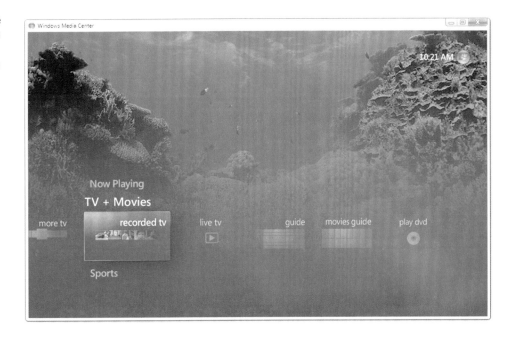

- It's a radio and an internet radio receiver.
- It's a digital video recorder that can record two channels at once – and it works with Freeview channels too.
- It's a door to a world of movie downloads, broadband TV and digital music.
- It's a home entertainment hub that can stream music to an Xbox 360.
- It's a games machine with graphics that consoles can only dream of.

Not bad for a humble PC, eh? However, to get the best from your PC's media features it's worth considering a few issues.

Think before you build it

A tower PC like the one we built in Part 3 might not be ideal for your living room, particularly if you're short of space or would prefer not to have a massive box in the corner. Noise is an issue too: a PC case with lots of fans can be very noisy and you don't want the quiet bits of a film spoiled by a PC that sounds like a jumbo jet. In many cases, you'd be better off with a small form factor PC like the one we built in Part 4, which is small enough to fit under your TV and quiet enough to do the job without spoiling your enjoyment.

Another option worth considering is a media centre case. Such cases are designed to blend in with the other equipment underneath your TV and, in addition to looking good, they're also designed to be quiet. In most cases you'll find that media centre cases follow the MicroATX standard, so there should be a wide selection of motherboards to choose from. Most of the major case manufacturers offer media centre cases and prices range from around £40 for a cheap and cheerful model to over £100 for something that looks like a really expensive hi-fi component.

Choose the right version of Windows

No matter which version of Vista or Windows 7 you go for you'll get Windows Media Player, which can copy CDs and turn them into digital music files. It can also play DVDs, connect to online music shops and it's the software you need for most video-on-demand services such as the ones offered by the BBC and Channel 4. However, if you're serious about your media PC it's worth going for the Home Premium or Ultimate editions, as these include some extra features including better video editing, DVD publishing software and best of all, Media Center. Media Center has been designed to work on big screens such as TVs, and if you want to use your PC without leaving the sofa it's well worth having. Rather annoyingly, Microsoft couldn't be bothered changing the spelling from Center to Centre when it created the UK versions of Windows.

Get a good TV tuner

Every PC with a DVD drive can play DVD movies, but if you want to use your PC to watch or record television then you'll need to invest in a TV tuner like the one we installed in our first PC project. We plumped for Hauppauge's Nova-T-500, which offers several useful features. First, it's a twin-tuner card, so you can watch one programme while recording another one (or record two programmes simultaneously). Second, it supports Freeview, so you can get digital channels from your existing TV aerial without investing in a satellite dish or cable subscription. Thirdly, it's an FM radio receiver and also supports digital audio stations over Freeview. Fourthly, it includes a remote control so you can stay on the sofa. And finally, it's cheap: at the time of writing, Amazon is selling it for around £60.

A TV tuner really makes the most of Windows Vista's media centre software and it means your PC can replace your video recorder, your DVD player and your Freeview box. We'd strongly recommend investing in a Freeview-compatible card, because over the next few years all of the existing analogue TV transmitters will be switched off. By around 2011 – or several years before then, depending on where you live – the only way to receive TV broadcasts without a satellite or cable TV service will be via Freeview.

Make the right connections

If you're using your PC as a living room media centre you'll need to make a few connections, and you might need to invest in a few cables too. You'll need to connect your sound card outputs to your stereo (or just use a dedicated set of good quality PC speakers); you'll need to connect your TV tuner card to your TV aerial; and you'll need to connect your PC's video card to your TV. With modern flat screen TVs that's usually straightforward, as most of them have either VGA connectors or DVI connectors that accept standard VGA or DVI cables. With older TVs you'll need to use your video card's TV-out connector.

Cut the cables

Cables aren't always a good thing, especially if they're trailing across your carpet. In addition to a remote control, a wireless keyboard and mouse is a good investment. Early models had shockingly bad battery life but these days, wireless peripherals run for weeks and weeks on a single set of batteries – and you can hide them when you're not using them. A wireless keyboard comes in particularly handy if you want to play games or surf the internet on your big-screen TV but don't fancy sitting with your nose pressed up against it.

Another option: the home hub

Sticking your PC under the TV isn't the only way to take advantage of its entertainment possibilities. You could make it the hub of a home entertainment network too. Don't worry, it's much simpler and cheaper than it sounds!

The idea behind a home hub is that your PC stores all your stuff, but other devices can access it. For example, if you've already got an Xbox 360 in the living room you can get it to share data with your PC, which means your Xbox can access your PC's music, your movies and your digital photo collection. Once again Windows Vista includes the necessary software, so both Windows Media Player and the Windows Vista Media Center can stream software to other PCs or to your Xbox 360.

For that software to work, though, you'll need a network connection between your Xbox and your PC. A wireless network is the obvious answer, but there are two potential problems with that. The first one is cost – the Xbox 360 wireless adapter doesn't come with the console and it's a rather pricey £60; if you don't already have a wireless router you'll need to buy one of them too – and the second one is that wireless networks aren't perfect. If your house is full of brick walls and other solid structures or your Xbox is located quite far away from your wireless networking adapter, you might find that the wireless signal is weak and that the connection speed suffers as a result. That's not a problem for streaming photos, but a patchy signal can seriously affect the quality of streaming music and render video unwatchable.

Even if you've got a perfect wireless signal, existing wireless kit isn't fast enough for really high quality video streaming – but that doesn't mean you need to start drilling holes and running Ethernet network cables everywhere. Thanks to powerline networking you can get Ethernet speeds without Ethernet cables.

Powerline networking is enormously clever. Instead of using wireless signals, it uses your house's electricity circuit to deliver network data. All you need is two adapters: one for your PC or router and one for your Xbox or second PC. Connect each adapter to the appropriate equipment (the cables you need come in the box) and then it's just a matter of plugging each one into a spare wall socket and switching it on. After around 20 seconds the adapters will connect to one another and you'll have faster-than-wireless networking speeds without any drilling or cable clutter.

Early powerline equipment was fairly slow, but current models are as fast as normal Ethernet networks. Look for devices offering speeds of 85Mbps or higher and, as ever, take such speeds with a pinch of salt: in the real world, you'll probably get speeds of around one-quarter to one-half of the quoted maximums. That's still much faster than wireless, though, and it's probably much faster than your broadband connection too. Expect to pay around £100 for a high-speed kit that includes everything you need to connect two devices.

If that's whetted your appetite for entertainment and you'd like to know even more, including alternative hardware and software options, check out our *PC Home Entertainment Manual*.

If you've got an Xbox 360, you can stream music, movies and photos to it from your Windows Vista PC over a wired or wireless network.

Powerline networking equipment transmits data via your house's existing electrical wiring. It's ideal for houses where wireless networks don't deliver.

Appendix 3
Beep and error codes

As we discussed on p.92 and p.151, the motherboard –
or more precisely, the BIOS chip on the motherboard –
emits a sequence of beeps whenever it identifies a
problem that is serious enough to prevent the computer
from starting normally. If the BIOS does manage to get
the computer up and running, it can also generate
onscreen error messages that help you identify trouble
spots. Here we reprint the codes used by AMI and
Award, makers of two commonly used BIOS programs.

Phoenix, another major player, uses a rather more complicated
scheme that is beyond our scope here.

AMI BIOS beep codes

Number of Beeps	Problem	Action
1	Memory refresh timer error.	Remove each memory module, clean the connecting edge that plugs into the motherboard socket, and replace. If that doesn't work, try restarting with a single memory module and see if you can identify the culprit by a process of elimination. If you still get the error code, replace with known good modules.
2	Parity error.	As with 1 beep above.
3	Main memory read/write test error.	As with 1 beep above.
4	Motherboard timer not operational.	Either the motherboard is faulty or one of the expansion cards has a problem. Remove all cards except the video card and restart. If the motherboard still issues this beep code, it has a serious, probably fatal problem. If the beeps stop, replace the cards one at a time and restart each time. This should identify the guilty party.
5	Processor error.	As with 4 beeps above.
6	Keyboard controller BAT test error.	As with 4 beeps above.
7	General exception error.	As with 4 beeps above.
8	Display memory error.	The video card is missing, faulty or incorrectly installed. Remove, clean the connecting contacts and replace. If that doesn't work, try using a different video card. If you are using integrated video instead of a video card, the motherboard may be faulty.
9	ROM checksum error.	As with 4 beeps above.
10	CMOS shutdown register read/write error.	As with 4 beeps above.
11	Cache memory bad.	As with 4 beeps above.

*AMIBIOS8 Checkpoint and Beep Code List version 1.2. Copyright of American Megatrends, Inc. Reprinted with permission.
All rights reserved.*

AMI BIOS error codes
Here are some examples of onscreen error messages:

Error	Action
Gate20 Error	The BIOS is unable to properly control the motherboard's Gate A20 function, which controls access of memory over 1MB. This may indicate a problem with the motherboard.
Multi-Bit ECC Error	This message will only occur on systems using ECC-enabled memory modules. ECC memory has the ability to correct single-bit errors that may occur from faulty memory modules. A multiple bit corruption of memory has occurred, and the ECC memory algorithm cannot correct it. This may indicate a defective memory module.
Parity Error	Fatal Memory Parity Error. System halts after displaying this message.
Boot Failure	This is a generic message indicating the BIOS could not boot from a particular device. This message is usually followed by other information concerning the device.
Invalid Boot Diskette	A diskette was found in the drive, but it is not configured as a bootable diskette.
Drive Not Ready	The BIOS was unable to access the drive because it indicated it was not ready for data transfer. This is often reported by drives when no media is present.
A: Drive Error	The BIOS attempted to configure the A: drive during POST, but was unable to properly configure the device. This may be because of a bad cable or faulty diskette drive.
Insert BOOT diskette in A:	The BIOS attempted to boot from the A: drive, but could not find a proper boot diskette.
Reboot and Select proper Boot device or Insert Boot Media in selected Boot device	BIOS could not find a bootable device in the system and/or removable media drive does not contain media.
NO ROM BASIC	This message occurs on some systems when no bootable device can be detected.
Primary Master Hard Disk Error	The IDE/ATAPI device configured as Primary Master could not be properly initialized by the BIOS. This message is typically displayed when the BIOS is trying to detect and configure IDE/ATAPI devices in POST.
Primary Slave Hard Disk Error	The IDE/ATAPI device configured as Primary Slave could not be properly initialized by the BIOS. This message is typically displayed when the BIOS is trying to detect and configure IDE/ATAPI devices in POST.
Secondary Master Hard Disk Error	The IDE/ATAPI device configured as Secondary Master could not be properly initialized by the BIOS. This message is typically displayed when the BIOS is trying to detect and configure IDE/ATAPI devices in POST.
Secondary Slave Hard Disk Error	The IDE/ATAPI device configured as Secondary Slave could not be properly initialized by the BIOS. This message is typically displayed when the BIOS is trying to detect and configure IDE/ATAPI devices in POST.

AMI BIOS error codes continued:

Error	Action
Primary Master Drive – ATAPI Incompatible	The IDE/ATAPI device configured as Primary Master failed an ATAPI compatibility test. This message is typically displayed when the BIOS is trying to detect and configure IDE/ATAPI devices in POST.
Primary Slave Drive – ATAPI Incompatible	The IDE/ATAPI device configured as Primary Slave failed an ATAPI compatibility test. This message is typically displayed when the BIOS is trying to detect and configure IDE/ATAPI devices in POST.
Secondary Master Drive – ATAPI Incompatible	The IDE/ATAPI device configured as Secondary Master failed an ATAPI compatibility test. This message is typically displayed when the BIOS is trying to detect and configure IDE/ATAPI devices in POST.
Secondary Slave Drive – ATAPI Incompatible	The IDE/ATAPI device configured as Secondary Slave failed an ATAPI compatibility test. This message is typically displayed when the BIOS is trying to detect and configure IDE/ATAPI devices in POST.
S.M.A.R.T. Capable but Command Failed	The BIOS tried to send a S.M.A.R.T. message to a hard disk, but the command transaction failed. This message can be reported by an ATAPI device using the S.M.A.R.T. error reporting standard. S.M.A.R.T. failure messages may indicate the need to replace the hard disk.
S.M.A.R.T. Command Failed	The BIOS tried to send a S.M.A.R.T. message to a hard disk, but the command transaction failed. This message can be reported by an ATAPI device using the S.M.A.R.T. error reporting standard. S.M.A.R.T. failure messages may indicate the need to replace the hard disk.
S.M.A.R.T. Status BAD, Backup and Replace	A S.M.A.R.T. capable hard disk sends this message when it detects an imminent failure. This message can be reported by an ATAPI device using the S.M.A.R.T. error reporting standard. S.M.A.R.T. failure messages may indicate the need to replace the hard disk.
S.M.A.R.T. Capable and Status BAD	A S.M.A.R.T. capable hard disk sends this message when it detects an imminent failure. This message can be reported by an ATAPI device using the S.M.A.R.T. error reporting standard. S.M.A.R.T. failure messages may indicate the need to replace the hard disk.
BootSector Write!!	The BIOS has detected software attempting to write to a drive's boot sector. This is flagged as possible virus activity. This message will only be displayed if Virus Detection is enabled in AMIBIOS Setup.
VIRUS: Continue (Y/N)?	If the BIOS detects possible virus activity, it will prompt the user. This message will only be displayed if Virus Detection is enabled in AMIBIOS Setup.
DMA-2 Error	Error initializing secondary DMA controller. This is a fatal error, often indicating a problem with system hardware.
DMA Controller Error	POST error while trying to initialize the DMA controller. This is a fatal error, often indicating a problem with system hardware.

AMI BIOS error codes continued:

Error	Action
CMOS Date/Time Not Set	The CMOS Date and/or Time are invalid. This error can be resolved by readjusting the system time in AMIBIOS Setup.
CMOS Battery Low	CMOS Battery is low. This message usually indicates that the CMOS battery needs to be replaced. It could also appear when the user intentionally discharges the CMOS battery.
CMOS Settings Wrong	CMOS settings are invalid. This error can be resolved by using AMIBIOS Setup.
CMOS Checksum Bad	CMOS contents failed the Checksum check. Indicates that the CMOS data has been changed by a program other than the BIOS or that the CMOS is not retaining its data due to malfunction. This error can typically be resolved by using AMIBIOS Setup.
Keyboard Error	Keyboard is not present or the hardware is not responding when the keyboard controller is initialized.
Keyboard/Interface Error	Keyboard Controller failure. This may indicate a problem with system hardware.
System Halted	The system has been halted. A reset or power cycle is required to reboot the machine. This message appears after a fatal error has been detected.

Award BIOS beep codes

Number of Beeps	Problem	Action
1 long beep followed by 2 short beeps	Video card problem	Remove the card, clean the connecting edge that plugs into the motherboard socket, and replace. If that doesn't work, try an alternative video card to establish whether the problem lies with the card or the AGP slot. If you are using integrated video instead of a video card, the motherboard may be faulty.
Any other beeps	Memory problem	Remove each memory module, clean the connecting edge that plugs into the motherboard socket, and replace. If that doesn't work, try restarting with a single memory module and see if you can identify the culprit by a process of elimination. If you still get the error code, replace with known good modules.

Award BIOS error codes Here are the standard Award onscreen error messages:

Error	Action
BIOS ROM checksum error – System halted	The checksum of the BIOS code in the BIOS chip is incorrect, indicating the BIOS code may have become corrupt. Contact your system dealer to replace the BIOS.
CMOS battery failed	The CMOS battery is no longer functional. Contact your system dealer for a replacement battery.
CMOS checksum error – Defaults loaded	Checksum of CMOS is incorrect, so the system loads the default equipment configuration. A checksum error may indicate that CMOS has become corrupt. This error may have been caused by a weak battery. Check the battery and replace if necessary.
CPU at nnnn	Displays the running speed of the CPU.
Display switch is set incorrectly	The display switch on the motherboard can be set to either monochrome or colour. This message indicates the switch is set to a different setting from that indicated in Setup. Determine which setting is correct, and then either turn off the system and change the jumper, or enter Setup and change the VIDEO selection.
Press ESC to skip memory test	The user may press Esc to skip the full memory test.
Floppy disk(s) fail	Cannot find or initialize the floppy drive controller or the drive. Make sure the controller is installed correctly. If no floppy drives are installed, be sure the Diskette Drive selection in Setup is set to NONE or AUTO.
HARD DISK initializing. Please wait a moment.	Some hard drives require extra time to initialize.
HARD DISK INSTALL FAILURE	Cannot find or initialize the hard drive controller or the drive. Make sure the controller is installed correctly. If no hard drives are installed, be sure the Hard Drive selection in Setup is set to NONE.
Hard disk(s) diagnosis fail	The system may run specific disk diagnostic routines. This message appears if one or more hard disks return an error when the diagnostics run.
Keyboard error or no keyboard present	Cannot initialize the keyboard. Make sure the keyboard is attached correctly and no keys are pressed during POST. To purposely configure the system without a keyboard, set the error halt condition in Setup to HALT ON ALL, BUT KEYBOARD. The BIOS then ignores the missing keyboard during POST.
Keyboard is locked out – Unlock the key	This message usually indicates that one or more keys have been pressed during the keyboard tests. Be sure no objects are resting on the keyboard.
Memory Test	This message displays during a full memory test, counting down the memory areas being tested.
Memory test fail	If POST detects an error during memory testing, additional information appears giving specifics about the type and location of the memory error.
Override enabled – Defaults loaded	If the system cannot boot using the current CMOS configuration, the BIOS can override the current configuration with a set of BIOS defaults designed for the most stable, minimal-performance system operations.
Press TAB to show POST screen	System OEMs may replace the Phoenix Technologies' AwardBIOS POST display with their own proprietary display. Including this message in the OEM display permits the operator to switch between the OEM display and the default POST display.
Primary master hard disk fail	POST detects an error in the primary master IDE hard drive.
Primary slave hard disk fail	POST detects an error in the secondary master IDE hard drive.
Secondary master hard disk fail	POST detects an error in the primary slave IDE hard drive.
Secondary slave hard disk fail	POST detects an error in the secondary slave IDE hard drive.

Appendix 4
Further resources

Here are some useful links that will lead you to more detailed information on selected subjects.

High Street retailers
Maplin	www.maplin.co.uk
PC World	www.pcworld.co.uk

Web/mail order retailers
Dabs	www.dabs.com/uk
Bosse Computers	www.bossecomputers.com
Tekheads	www.tekheads.co.uk
Overclockers	www.overclockers.co.uk
Quiet PC	www.quietpc.com/uk

Computer fair contacts
Computer Fairs Information	www.computerfairs.co.uk
Northern Computer Markets	www.computermarkets.co.uk
Computer Markets Online	www.computermarketsonline.co.uk
The Show Guide	www.theshowguide.co.uk
All-Formats Computer Fairs	www.afm96.co.uk
The Best Event	www.bestevent.co.uk
Abacus Computer Fairs	www.fairs.co.uk

B-grade retailers
Morgan Computers	www.morgancomputers.co.uk
Dabs	www.dabs.com/uk/channels/Usedclearance
IT Dealers	www.itdealers.co.uk/catalog/index.php

High street and web retailers also sell-off B-grade stock from time to time; look for bargain bins, manager's specials and the like.

Consumer rights information
Trading Standards Institute	www.tradingstandards.gov.uk
Office of Fair Trading	www.oft.gov.uk

Processor manufacturers
Intel	www.intel.com
AMD	www.amd.com

Chipset information
Intel	www.intel.com
AMD	www.amd.com
ALi	www.ali.com.tw
VIA	www.via.com.tw
SiS	www.sis.com
Nvidia	www.nvidia.com

Intel and AMD also publish lists of motherboards that are compatible with their processors:
Intel	http://indigo.intel.com/mbsg/
AMD	http://snipurl.com/drwp

Memory information
Crucial Technology	http://support.crucial.com
Kingston Technology	www.kingston.com/ukroot
Rambus	www.rambus.com

Utilities

Intel Chipset Identification Utility
www.intel.com/support/chipsets/inf/chipsetid.htm

Sandra	www.sisoftware.co.uk
Ontrack JumperViewer	www.ontrack.com/jumperviewer

Audio technology

Dolby Labs	www.dolby.com
DTS	www.dtsonline.com
Steinberg	www.steinberg.net
THX	www.thx.com
DirectX	www.microsoft.com/windows/directx

Graphics technology

Nvidia	www.nvidia.com
ATI	www.ati.com
Matrox	www.matrox.com

CD/DVD technology

CD-Recordable FAQ	www.cdrfaq.org
DVD Demystified	www.dvddemystified.com
DVD+RW Alliance	www.dvdrw.com
DVD Forum	www.dvdforum.org

Hardware review sites

Tom's Hardware Guide	www.tomshardware.com
Motherboards.org	www.motherboards.org
ExtremeTech	www.extremetech.com
Anand Tech	www.anandtech.com
Digital-Daily	www.digital-daily.com

BIOS updates and information

Phoenix	www.phoenix.com
Award	www.unicore.com
AMI	www.megatrends.com
Bios-Drivers	www.bios-drivers.com

Manufacturers featured

Gigabyte	http://uk.giga-byte.com
AOpen	www.aopen.nl
Crucial Technology	www.crucial.com/uk/index.asp
Kingston technology	www.kingston.com/ukroot
Seagate	www.seagate.com
Mitsumi	www.mitsumi.de
Creative Labs	www.europe.creative.com
Lite-On	www.liteonit.com
Zalman	www.zalmanusa.com
Lian-Li	www.bossecomputers.com
US Robotics	www.usr-emea.com

Software featured

Windows Vista	www.microsoft.com
OpenOffice.org	www.openoffice.org
Google Docs & Spreadsheets	http://docs.google.com
AVAST antivirus	www.avast.com
AVG antivirus	http://free.grisoft.com
ClamWin AV	www.clamwin.com
Trillian	www.trillian.cc

All you ever wanted to know about ...

Form factors	www.formfactors.org
Serial ATA	www.serialata.org
Wireless networking	www.wi-fi.org
PCI Express	www.pcisig.com

Appendix 5
Abbreviations & acronyms

A handy list of some shorthand terms used throughout
this manual or that you might otherwise encounter.

2D/3D	Two-dimensional/three-dimensional
2x/4x, etc.	Double-speed/quadruple-speed, etc.
A3D	Aureal 3D
AC '97	Audio Codec '97
AGP	Accelerate Graphics Port
AMR	Audio Modem Riser
ASIO	Audio Stream In/Out
ATA	Advanced Technology Attachment
ATAPI	Advanced Technology Attachment Packet Interface
ATX	Advanced Technology Extended
BIOS	Basic In/Out System
CD	Compact Disc
CD-DA	Compact Disc – Digital Audio
CD-R	Compact Disc – Recordable
CD-ROM	Compact Disc – Read-Only Memory
CD-RW	Compact Disc – Rewriteable
CMOS	Complementary Metal-Oxide Semiconductor
CNR	Communications and Networking Riser
CPU	Central Processing Unit
CRIMM	Continuity Rambus Inline Memory Module
DAE	Digital Audio Extraction
dB	Decibel
DDR-RAM	Double Data Rate – Random-Access Memory
DIMM	Dual Inline Memory Module
DMA	Direct Memory Access
DSL	Digital Subscriber Line
DTS	Digital Theatre Systems
DVD	Digital Versatile Disc
DVD-RAM	Digital Versatile Disc – Random-Access Memory
DVD-ROM	Digital Versatile Disc – Read-Only Memory
DVD-R/RW	Digital Versatile Disc – Recordable/Rewriteable
DVD+R/RW	Digital Versatile Disc – Recordable/Rewriteable
DVI	Digital Visual Interface
EAX	Environmental Audio Extensions
FAQ	Frequently Asked Questions
FAT	File Allocation Table
FSB	Front Side Bus
GB	Gigabyte
GPU	Graphics Processing Unit
HDD	Hard Disk Drive
HT	Hyper-Threading
I/O	Input/Output
ICH	Integrated Controller Hub
IDE	Integrated Drive Electronics
IEC	International Electrotechnical Commission
IEEE	Institute of Electrical and Electronic Engineers
ISA	Industry Standard Architecture
KB	Kilobyte
KHz	Kilohertz
LAN	Local Area Network
LED	Light-Emitting Diode
LGA	Land Grid Array
MB	Megabyte
Mbps	Megabits per second
MCH	Memory Controller Hub
MHz	Megahertz
MIDI	Musical Instrument Digital Interface
MP3	Motion Picture Experts Group Audio Layer Three
MPEG	Motion Picture Experts Group
NIC	Network Interface Card
NTFS	New Technology File System
Pentium 4	Pentium 4
PC	Personal Computer
PCI	Peripheral Component Interconnect
PDA	Personal Digital Assistant
PDF	Portable Document Format
PnP	Plug-and-Play
POST	Power On Self Test
PS/2	Personal System/2
PSU	Power Supply Unit
RAID	Redundant Array of Independent Disks
RAM	Random-Access Memory
RIMM	Rambus Inline Memory Module
S.M.A.R.T.	Self-Monitoring Analysis and Reporting Technology
SATA	Serial Advanced Technology Attachment
SCSI	Small Computer Systems Interface
SD-RAM	Synchronous Dynamic – Random-Access Memory
SPDIF	Sony/Philips Digital Interface
TFT	Thin Film Transistor
THX	Tomlinson Holman Experiment
UPS	Uninterruptible Power Supply
USB	Universal Serial Port
VGA	Video Graphics Array
Wi-Fi	Wireless Fidelity
ZIF	Zero Insertion Force

Index

Authors	**Kyle MacRae and Gary Marshall**
Copy Editor	**Shena Deuchars**
Photography	**Iain McLean**
Front cover illustration	**Digital Progression**
Page build	**James Robertson**
Index	**Shena Deuchars**
Project Manager	**Louise McIntyre**